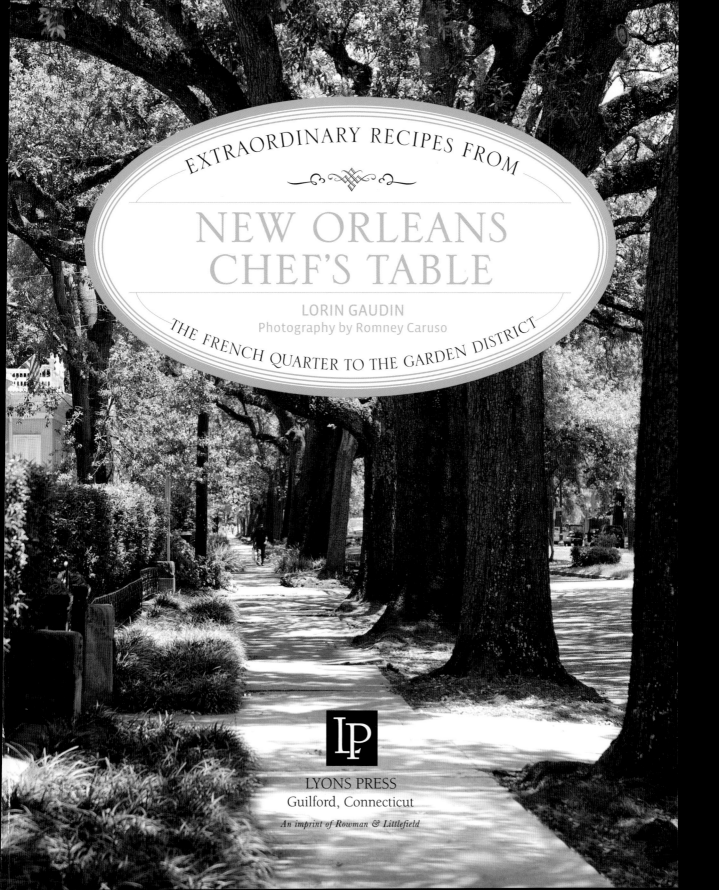

EXTRAORDINARY RECIPES FROM

NEW ORLEANS
CHEF'S TABLE

LORIN GAUDIN
Photography by Romney Caruso

THE FRENCH QUARTER TO THE GARDEN DISTRICT

LYONS PRESS
Guilford, Connecticut

An imprint of Rowman & Littlefield

Lyons Press is an imprint of Rowman & Littlefield.

All photography by Romney Caruso, with the exception of the author photo on page 194 by Remy Gaudin

Distributed by NATIONAL BOOK NETWORK

Library of Congress Cataloging-in-Publication Data is available on file.

ISBN 978-0-7627-8140-9

Printed in the United States of America

Restaurants and chefs often come and go, and menus are ever-changing. We recommend you call ahead to obtain current information before visiting any of the establishments in this book.

This book is dedicated to the City of New Orleans . . . a place that took me in, embraced me hard, and slipped deep into my soul to become an indelible part of my DNA and my home. I love New Orleans—the people, the music, the culture, and of course, the food— and I am grateful she loved me right back.

Acknowledgments

I want to thank first and foremost my husband Andre and sons Collins and Remy, who all tolerate my food craziness, the constant chatter, piles of cookbooks, obsession with food and cooking, and who have supported me unfailingly in all my culinary endeavors. I must thank my sisters and brother for being as food-crazy as me and always letting me in on the latest and greatest places to eat where they live—it gives me a great national perspective. My mom and dad get thanks for the genetics that made me who I am and am not. I also want to thank my dear departed mother-in-law, Janice, who was so special to me and taught me many family recipes that stretch back more than a hundred years. She would be proud to know that those dishes remain an important part of Gaudin meal rituals. To my photographer, Romney, whose talent, energy, excitement, and hunger made this project pop with color and taste: I am in awe. It is said that we eat with our eyes first, and Romney's drool-inducing food photographs prove that perfectly. Finally, I am forever grateful to the gob-smackingly brilliant and fun chefs of New Orleans, who bring tears to my eyes with their stunning art and whom I adore.

Contents

Introduction

In New Orleans, we can be eating a meal while talking about another meal or cooking or restaurants, and simultaneously planning the next meal. Food obsessed, that's what we are.

—Everyone in New Orleans

It is well established that New Orleanians are food obsessed. Some say that food is our lingua franca, the way we communicate, our working language, the way we connect to one another. And that is the absolute truth. It is the norm to hear tables of diners talking food, cooking, favored restaurants, new restaurants, the demise of beloved restaurants, the next restaurant, markets, local products, and food finds—all with a mouth full of food from the plate immediately on the table. The spirit of New Orleans is reflected in her cooking and restaurants, her people, and her multiplicity of cultures.

The city has long been known for certain foods and dishes—beignets, jambalaya, gumbo, boudin, crawfish—our regional cuisine, what the national food press has called New Orleans's "one menu." It is true that we do have that menu, and we do it proudly and beautifully, but New Orleans is in a very exciting transitional time for food. We have more, do more, explore more, and have created a bunch of "menus" deserving of attention. No one has abandoned tradition in the name of progress—the two walk hand in hand. We embrace our food traditions, eat lovingly and happily from a plate of red beans and rice or let the juices run down our arms from a messy roast beef po-boy, but that doesn't stop us from diving into compressed melon and icy-cool avocado "dippin' dots"; we're immersed in it, deeply. I don't believe that any of our foods is threatened with extinction—we're too stubborn and love ourselves too much to let that happen. Food here is revered religiously and consumed passionately. Radio host, author, and food personality Tom Fitzmorris reported that in 2005 there were just over 800 sit-down restaurants in the New Orleans area. Continuing to keep count, Mr. Fitzmorris recently reported that we have more than 1,300 restaurants (and growing), although our population hasn't returned to what it was in 2005! Fewer people and almost twice as many restaurants! That's a phenomenon in and of itself.

Yes, we love our food. We love the Gulf that gives us an incredible variety of finfish, crab, shrimp, and oysters, our waterways and rice fields from which spring crawfish, our alluvial soil that gives glorious Creole tomatoes with their stunning sunshine-bright flavor. We adore our elders and families who cook and remind us of important recipes: the flame

keepers who gather in organizations, open museums, and offer exhibits and collections for us to experience, so we never forget a sip or a bite. And New Orleans is experiencing a culinary evolution too. As the template of our city shifts, grows and renovates, restores and reinvigorates, so do the food, cooking, and restaurants.

The new New Orleans is a fascinating place. Natives and long-standing transplants stand shoulder-to-shoulder with the new locals, and there is no denying a decidedly younger demographic who contribute a fresh look and palate. Many adventurous cooks, chefs and those clamoring to be restaurant owners, have successfully taken the leap into the industry, in parts of New Orleans that were previously quiet or undeveloped. This book covers some of everything—well-loved "grande dame" restaurants, places that have been around and refreshed, places that have made a local mark on our restaurant landscape but aren't as well known, and those that are brand new.

New Orleans is nestled in the Parish of Orleans, positioned on the crescent of the Mississippi River and mapped by neighborhoods. Each of these neighborhoods has a distinct tone, and all are filled cheek-by-jowl with historic homes—mansions and shotguns, pristine or time- and weather-worn, many family-owned for hundreds of years—mixed with commerce. It is a New Orleans hallmark that neighborhoods are both residential and commercial. The architectural styles reflect Spanish and French rule as well as accommodations to our tropical climate that swelters in summer and withstands the vagaries of catastrophic storms.

ORGANIZATION

This book is structured according to some of the better-known New Orleans neighborhoods—this city of neighborhoods. Obviously not every neighborhood is covered, but those in this book cut a wide swath from the Garden District, winding through Uptown and Carrollton into Mid-City, next traveling to the Marigny and Bywater, then rolling into the French Quarter and on into Downtown and Central Business District, which then becomes the Arts and Warehouse District. It's a delicious tour of our dining and local culture. New Orleans is a sensorial place, with very specific identifying aromas that signify. The spicy scent of cayenne, herbs, and lemon means crawfish, crab, or shrimp season, while the air thick with fried chicken's pungent, mouthwateringly greasy scent is all about Mardi Gras (or "Carnival" if you're a native). There's the dusty sagelike aroma of swamp bay that hangs on the dark of sultry summer evenings, and of course the musty, wet-wood funk of neighborhood bars that beg for an icy beer or soothing highball. By engaging all five senses, it is possible to see, hear, feel, smell, and taste the distinguishing differences throughout New Orleans. New Orleans is intensely tactile; even walking Jackson Square can evoke the sound of nineteenth-century heels clicking on the slate, or cause the weighty layers of historic events both glorious and heart-wrenching to be felt on the skin. Food, dining, and cuisine are a natural extension of the experience—yes, New Orleans is an experience—filled with people often referred to as characters. New Orleans is a living story. And this is my version.

This book is about my love for the chefs and restaurants of New Orleans, about the beauty that is Louisiana product, smarts, creativity, and deliciousness. It's about the new way we are eating right now in New Orleans, dispelling that one-menu moniker, screaming from the rooftops that while we love our culinary traditions, there is more going on here. Come visit, wander the neighborhoods, and dine extensively and comprehensively—it's so worth it. Try the dishes for which we are famous, or today's interpretations; the ethnic foods; the food trucks; the produce and bites at the Crescent City Farmers Market. This is a delicious city, my home. Come fall head-over-heels in love, a deep foodie love, with New Orleans. And if you can't visit, then cook up a recipe or two and savor the flavor. You'll fall in love just the same.

THE GARDEN DISTRICT
&
LOWER GARDEN DISTRICT

Commander's Palace

1403 Washington Avenue
(504) 899-8221
commanderspalace.com
Executive Chef: Tory McPhail

The Garden District of New Orleans is a lovely place, filled with grand mansions, old families, and one of our city's grandest "grande dames." The post–Hurricane Katrina renovation of Commander's continues to lend elegance, but there is also a more approachable feeling to the place. Executive Chef Tory McPhail enhances that vibration. Of course the restaurant continues to serve its amazing turtle soup and its bread pudding souffle—the world would be lost without them—but there are also Tory's bolder explorations and cooking fancies that appear on the menu to bring a freshness reflecting progress without abandoning tradition. Chef Tory and the Commander's Palace owners, Miss Ella, her daughter Ti Martin, and her cousin Lally Brennan, exude charm, grace, and fun. The cocktails have a kick, thanks to the Cocktail Chicks (Ti and Lally) and the stellar bar team. Everything is sourced locally, regionally, and/or from the United States; that's long been the way things are done, and now Commander's Palace does things with a current feel. A 25-cent-martini lunch, anyone?

CRAWFISH BOIL VICHYSSOISE

(YIELDS 1 GALLON/20 PORTIONS; MAY BE HALVED)

For the soup:

8 ounces boiled crawfish, pureed

2½ pounds red bliss or any thin-skinned, small new
potatoes

4 ounces leeks, green tops removed, washed well and
sliced

4 ounces carrots, peeled and chopped

4 ounces celery, stalks only, washed and chopped

1 ounce Zatarain's crawfish boil powder

3 quarts whole milk

1 ounce sugarcane vinegar

For the garnish:

1 pound button mushrooms, in small dice

1 pound corn kernels

4 ounces garlic cloves, peeled

4 ounces sweet potatoes, in small dice

3 pounds crawfish tails, lightly grilled

20 whole boiled crawfish

2 ounces red chili oil

To make the soup: Combine all ingredients in a
pot and bring to a simmer. Cook for 40 minutes
or until potatoes are cooked through and very
tender. Working in small batches, puree the soup
in a high-powered blender until very smooth
and creamy. Pass through a chinoise and adjust
thickness and seasoning as necessary. This soup
is intended to be served at room temperature.

To garnish the soup: Prepare a bubbling pot of
crawfish boil, and an ice bath of crawfish boil
water. Blanch the mushrooms, corn, garlic, and
sweet potatoes separately in the crawfish boil
until al dente, and then shock them in the ice
bath to stop the cooking. Combine with the
crawfish tails and spoon into soup bowls. Pour
6 ounces of soup around the garnish and place
a whole boiled crawfish on top. Finish by adding
tiny drops of chili oil to the surface of the soup
for added kick.

GULF SHRIMP & BLUE CRAB ENCHILADAS
(SERVES 8 AS APPETIZER, 4 AS ENTREE)

For the enchilada sauce:

8 tomatoes, chopped
1 onion, diced
1 chipotle chile, soaked for 10 minutes in warm water
1 teaspoon cayenne pepper
½ bunch cilantro
½ cup vinegar
1 teaspoon ground cumin
2 cloves garlic
Salt to taste

For the enchiladas:

4 teaspoons butter
2 cloves garlic, minced
1 large onion, diced
2 jalapeños, seeds removed, diced
2 large tomatoes, diced
Kernels from 1 ear of corn
1 cup cooked black beans
½ bunch cilantro
16 shrimp (36/40 count), peeled, deveined, and chopped
½ pound blue crab meat, picked free of shell
½ teaspoon ground cumin
½ teaspoon ground coriander
Salt and pepper to taste
2 cups corn oil
8 corn tortillas
2 cups enchilada sauce
8 ounces Idiazabal cheese, grated

To make the sauce: Place all ingredients in heavy saucepan with 2 cups water and cook for 20 minutes on medium heat. Remove from heat and puree in blender until smooth. Season with salt to your liking.

To make the enchiladas: Place a large sauté pan on medium heat. Add butter to pan. Add garlic, onion, jalapeños, and tomatoes. Sauté until onions are translucent. Add corn, beans, and cilantro. Cook for 4 to 5 minutes. Add shrimp and crab and cook for 2 to 3 minutes. Add cumin and coriander and then season with salt and pepper. Allow to cool.

Preheat oven to 375°F. Heat the corn oil to 275°F in large pot. Dip each tortilla in the warm oil for 15 seconds or until it is pliable, then coat it in enchilada sauce. Place 3 ounces of shrimp and crab filling on the tortilla and roll into a cylinder. Place in a heatproof dish.

When all tortillas are filled, sprinkle with cheese and more sauce. Bake for 5 to 7 minutes or until cheese melts.

"Compressed" Strawberries

(SERVES 4)

For the strawberries:

24 Ponchatoula strawberries, hulled
1 cup strawberry jam

For the Jell-O pearls:

2 cups vegetable oil
1 package strawberry Jell-O

For the whipped cream:

1 cup heavy cream
½ cup strawberry jam

For the strawberry Hurricane cocktail:

1 ounce light rum
1 ounce dark rum
1 ounce pineapple juice
1 ounce orange juice
2 ounces strawberry jam

For assembly:

Compressed strawberries, halved
Strawberry whipped cream
4 ounces strawberry Jell-O pearls
1 package strawberry Pop Rocks
4 strawberry Pixy Stix
4 ounces strawberry Hurricane cocktail
4 fresh mint sprigs
Powdered sugar in a shaker

To compress the strawberries: Place the berries in a medium bowl, rinse briefly under cool tap water, and drain very well. Add 1 cup of the strawberry jam and toss to coat evenly. Place the berries in a heavy Cryovac bag and vacuum-seal it. Break the seal on the corner of the bag and reseal 2 more times to drive the jam into

the inside of the berry. Finally, after the third compression, leave the bag sealed for 4 hours to marinate.

To make the pearls: Place vegetable oil in the freezer in a shallow baking dish and chill for 1 to 2 hours. Prepare strawberry-flavored Jell-O according to package instructions, temper it in an ice bath, and stir constantly with a rubber spatula until it just starts to get thick. The Jell-O should be about 50 to 60°F. Pour the thickened jelly into a squeeze bottle with a narrow tip. Remove the chilled oil from the freezer and place on a countertop. Working back and forth and about 1 foot above the surface of the oil, inject the Jell-O into the oil to form tiny pearls. Pour the Jell-O and oil through a fine strainer to separate. Drain for 5 minutes in the refrigerator so the pearls are very dry and free of oil.

To make the whipped cream: Pour cream and ½ cup of strawberry jam into a bowl and whisk quickly to thicken. Note that different brands of jam have different sugar content, so adjust amount as necessary.

To make the strawberry Hurricane: Place all ingredients into an ice-filled cocktail shaker. Shake well to blend the cocktail and dissolve the jam. Strain.

To assemble: Break the seal of the compressed strawberries, pour them into a bowl, and slice each berry in half. Smear the strawberry whipped cream in the center of four dessert plates. Arrange the sliced berries, cut side up, along the whipped cream, then garnish the tops with the pearls, Pop Rocks, and Pixy Stix. Place a small hurricane glass on each plate and pour in the cocktail. Finish with mint sprigs and a light dusting of powdered sugar.

Coquette

2800 Magazine Street
(504) 265-0421
COQUETTE-NOLA.COM
Executive Chef: Michael Stoltzfus

Washington Avenue at Magazine Street is a busy corner. Chef Michael Stoltzfus and business partner Lillian Hubbard took over this 1880s-era building in 2008, after it had served as home to several businesses, including a few restaurants that just didn't stick. Obviously Chef Michael has the glue that works, because since the day he opened the doors, the place has been busy and gets great buzz. The bar is a centerpiece, with cleverly crafted cocktails, and the food is refined by easygoing. Chef Michael is a proponent of the locally sourced movement for his "American cuisine," and his vegetable dishes exemplify that love and care. Coquette's pastry chef Zak Miller is a gem. He gets as smart and playful with his desserts as Chef Michael does with the cuisine. They are a solid team, and they both get a big bang out of the monthly pop-up dinners that showcase even more of their playful side with only slightly more casual fare. The Fried Chicken and Bourbon Dinner was a big hit.

Roasted Carrots

(SERVES 2)

For the caraway crumble:

¾ cup all-purpose flour
¾ cup almond flour
⅔ cup powdered sugar
¾ cup unsalted butter, cut into cubes
3 teaspoons ground caraway

For the ginger aioli:

1 egg
Juice of 1 lemon
1 garlic clove
1-inch piece of fresh ginger, peeled
1 cup olive oil
Salt to taste

For the ginger butter:

3 tablespoons minced fresh ginger
1½ cups unsalted butter
1 bunch chives, minced
Salt to taste

For the baby carrots:

10 baby carrots
4 teaspoons ginger butter
½ teaspoon salt
Flat-leaf parsley, for garnish
Leaves from celery heart, for garnish

To make the crumble: Preheat oven to 250°F. Fit a stand mixer with the paddle attachment and place all the ingredients in the bowl. Mix until fully incorporated. Press into a thin layer, about ½ inch, onto a baking sheet lined with parchment paper. Bake until dark brown and dry, about 45 minutes.

To make the aioli: In a food processor place the egg, lemon juice, garlic, and ginger. With the motor running, slowly add the olive oil, creating an emulsion. Taste and season with salt as needed.

To make the ginger butter: In a stand mixer with a paddle attachment, mix all ingredients until incorporated, about 1 minute.

To cook the carrots: In a sauté pan place the carrots, ginger butter, salt, and enough water to cover. Simmer on low heat until carrots are almost tender throughout. There should be very little water left, and the carrots should be glazed. If there is still water left and the carrots are tender, remove the carrots and slowly reduce the liquid in the pan until it is thickened. Return the carrots to the pan and roast in a 350°F oven for 5 minutes, shaking the pan every couple of minutes. They should be lightly browned.

To plate: On each plate place a few dollops of aioli, about 1 tablespoon. Add one-quarter of the caraway crumble around and on top of the aioli. Place the roasted carrots on top of the crumble. Garnish with flat-leaf parsley and celery heart leaves.

CHEESECAKE ICE CREAM SANDWICH
(SERVES 8)

For the graham cracker sablée:

1¾ cups butter
1 vanilla bean
⅓ cup honey
¼ cup brown sugar
3 egg yolks
1¼ cups whole wheat flour
⅔ cup all-purpose flour
1 teaspoon salt
1 tablespoon cinnamon sugar

For the blueberry compote:

½ cup brown sugar
4¼ cups blueberries
2 vanilla beans
Zest of 1 orange
1 cinnamon stick
1 teaspoon five-spice powder

For the cheesecake semifreddo:

2 cups sugar
15 egg yolks
4¼ cups cream
2 pounds cream cheese, at room temperature
2 teaspoons vanilla
Zest of 1 lemon
Pinch of salt

To make the sablée: Cream together the butter with the vanilla, honey, and brown sugar. Add the egg yolks and mix to combine. Sift the two flours and salt, and add to the butter mixture. Wrap the dough in plastic wrap and chill for 4 hours or overnight.

Preheat oven to 300°F. Roll dough to ¼ inch thick and cut out rounds the same diameter as the molds you will use for the cheesecake. Brush lightly with water and sprinkle with cinnamon sugar. Bake for 15 to 20 minutes or until deep golden brown.

To make the compote: Caramelize the brown sugar in a dry pan (it will melt and look like peanut butter), stirring constantly. Add the remaining ingredients and cook until the mixture thickens and all the sugar has dissolved. Remove the vanilla bean. Cool.

To make the cheesecake semifreddo: Place the sugar and 7 ounces water in a small pot. Cook to 250°F. Meanwhile start whipping the yolks on high in a stand mixer. When the sugar reaches the proper temperature, slowly pour it into the whipping yolks. Whip till cool. In a chilled bowl, whip the cream to soft peaks and set aside. Mix the cream cheese with the vanilla, lemon zest, and salt until soft. Fold the yolk mixture into the cream cheese mixture, then fold in the whipped cream. Pipe the mixture into fleximolds or any round molds, and freeze.

To assemble: When the semifreddo is frozen, unmold and place between two of the graham cracker sablée rounds. Serve on a bed of blueberry compote.

Emeril's Delmonico

1300 Saint Charles Avenue
(504) 525-4937
emerilsrestaurants.com/emerils-delmonico
Executive Chef: Emeril Lagasse

When Chef Emeril bought the old-time restaurant space called Delmonico, those New Orleanians who were of an age were shaken. As is the way here, the thought of change didn't sit well. Ah, but we're talking about Emeril Lagasse, and what resulted was a stunningly renovated and restored building that caters to fine dining, in the way the original Delmonico envisioned, only a tad more contemporary Creole with some global inspiration. Meats are aged on the premises, and the menu features big cuts of beef, as well as lamb, duck, and fish plucked from the Gulf. The cocktail lounge is fun, with live music on the weekends and great Sazeracs to sip.

EMERIL'S DELMONICO PORK CHEEKS WITH CREOLE DIRTY RICE

RECIPE COURTESY EMERIL LAGASSE,
EMERIL'S FOOD OF LOVE PRODUCTIONS, 2008

(SERVES 4)

2½ pounds pork cheeks, cleaned and trimmed of all
    tough membranes
8 cloves garlic
6 sprigs fresh thyme
1½ tablespoons kosher salt
1 tablespoon coarsely ground black pepper
1 tablespoon coriander seeds
Vegetable oil as needed
1 cup flour, or more as needed for dusting
2 tablespoons unsalted butter
1 recipe Creole Dirty Rice, for serving (recipe follows)

Preheat the oven to 325°F.

Place the pork cheeks, garlic, thyme, salt,
pepper, and coriander seeds in a baking dish
just large enough to hold the pork in one layer.
Add enough vegetable oil to completely cover
the pork. Cover the dish tightly with aluminum foil
and bake until cheeks are fork-tender, usually 4
to 4½ hours. (This will depend on the size of the
pork cheeks you are able to procure, so check
periodically during the cooking time.) When the
pork is tender, remove from the oven and allow
to cool in the oil. Once cool, remove the cheeks
from the oil and pat dry with paper towels. (Oil
may be strained and used for another purpose.)

Dust the cheeks lightly with flour. Heat a medium
sauté pan over medium-high heat. When hot,
add 2 tablespoons of oil to the pan, and when
oil is hot, add 1 tablespoon of the butter. Sauté
the cheeks, in batches if necessary, until golden
brown on all sides, 2 to 3 minutes. Remove

from the pan and repeat with remaining cheeks,
adding more vegetable oil and remaining butter if
necessary.

Serve the cheeks hot, with the Creole Dirty Rice.

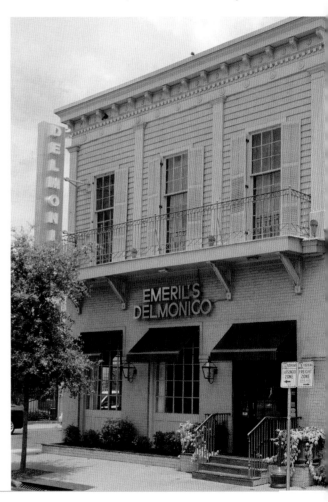

CREOLE DIRTY RICE

RECIPE COURTESY EMERIL LAGASSE,
EMERIL'S FOOD OF LOVE PRODUCTIONS, 2008

(SERVES 4)

1 tablespoon vegetable oil

1 tablespoon butter

½ cup chopped yellow onion

½ cup chopped bell pepper

¼ pound ground pork

¼ pound chicken livers, pureed

2 bay leaves

1 tablespoon finely chopped jalapeño

½ teaspoon salt

¼ teaspoon ground coriander

¼ teaspoon ground cumin

¼ teaspoon cayenne

2 cups cooked long grain white rice

¼ cup beef stock or canned low-sodium beef broth

Dash of Tabasco, or other Louisiana hot sauce, or
to taste

In a large skillet, heat the oil over medium-high heat. When hot, add the butter, onions, and bell peppers and sauté vegetables until tender and lightly caramelized, 4 to 6 minutes. Add the pork and cook, using the spoon to break the pork into small pieces, until well browned, 1 to 2 minutes. Add the liver puree, bay leaves, jalapeno, salt, coriander, cumin, and cayenne and cook until liver is cooked through and spices are fragrant, 2 to 3 minutes. Add the rice and beef stock and continue to cook, stirring, until well combined and heated through, 2 to 3 minutes longer. Adjust the seasoning if necessary and add hot sauce to taste.

Irish House

1432 Saint Charles Avenue
(504) 595-6755
THEIRISHHOUSENEWORLEANS.COM
Executive Chef: Matt Murphy

When Chef Matt Murphy bought the building on the corner of Saint Charles and Melpomene, he knew what he wanted to do: turn it into a traditional Irish pub. An Irishman himself, Chef Matt concentrated on the gigantic bar and beer taps. Seating is converted church pews, the walls are covered in Irish and sports ephemera. It's a lively atmosphere with sports on the televisions, traditional music on the stereo, a cool retail shop to buy UK candies, rugby jerseys, and all kinds of Irish treats sweet and savory. There's also a cozy fireplace seating area and lots of food. On the menu are traditional Irish dishes like shepherd's pie, fish and chips, and chicken curry with chips. "I wanted to offer pub food like I can get back home—and a properly poured Guinness," says Chef Matt. There are also a few Louisiana nods like the Murphinator Poboy of thinly sliced roast beef, french fries, and Crystal onion rings topped with Boursin aioli and served with dipping gravy. In addition to live music, parties, and lunch and dinner, there's a weekend brunch for an Irish breakfast of rashers, eggs, potatoes, tomatoes, black and white puddings, sautéed mushrooms, and baked beans. Make no mistake, Chef Matt is proud of his Irish roots, but he displays a lot of local love, and he's loved right back.

AUTUMN IRISH CHANNEL BEEF STEW

(SERVES 8)

2 ounces vegetable oil
2 pounds stewing beef, cubed
Salt and pepper
¼ cup flour
2 medium onions, sliced
½ head celery, diced
2 medium carrots, peeled and cut into half moons
2 small leeks, diced
2 bay leaves
1 large sprig thyme
1 small sprig rosemary
1 gallon beef stock
1 pint NOLA Irish Channel stout
4 potatoes, peeled and cubed
Chopped parsley, for garnish

Use a heavy-gauge pot. Set the temperature on high and add oil. Season the beef with salt and pepper. Then toss the beef and the flour together. Add the beef to the pot and allow it to brown. Stir in the onions, celery, carrots, and leeks along with the herbs, stock, and stout. Bring to a boil and then allow the stew to cook for about 1 to 1¼ hours.

Add the potatoes and cook for another 40 minutes or until tender.

To serve, remove the bay leaves, thyme, and rosemary. Taste and adjust seasoning with salt and pepper. Garnish with chopped parsley.

La Divina Gelateria

3005 Magazine Street, (504) 342-2634
621 Saint Peter Street, (504) 302-2692
Loyola University, (504) 258-2115
ladivinagelateria.com
Executive Chef: Mia Calamia
Owners: Katrina and Carmelo Turillo

While living in Italy, owners Katrina and Carmelo Turillo were entranced by the Italians' simple, joyful lifestyle that includes the passeggiata, an evening stroll where people pour onto the streets to meander, chat with friends and neighbors, then cap the evening with a scoop of gelato. With that in mind, and after traveling across Italy to study the artisanal method of gelato and sorbetto making, the Turillos brought their skill back to New Orleans to open La Divina Gelateria in 2007. Their product focus is all natural, local, and organic whenever possible, and the flavors epitomize what's in season—Strawberry Balsamic sorbetto in April and May, Blueberry Basil in June, Peach & Prosecco in July, and so on. There are both straightforward and creative gelato flavors like Pistachio, Aztec Chocolate, or Bourbon-Pecan. Panini are made in the classic Italian tradition with fresh, top-quality ingredients on locally baked, crusty bread, and Chef Mia Calamia has expanded the overall selection by adding a few gluten-free baked goods, more panini (a favorite is the porchetta, served with seasonal mostarda), and freshly made soups. Their espresso is top notch and just a thing of beauty tipped over a scoop of plain vanilla gelato, known as an affogato. The gelato recipe here is one of the shop's most popular.

CRÈME BRÛLÉE GELATO

(SERVES 6)

For the crème:

½ cup cream
2¾ cups whole milk
5 egg yolks
¾ cup sugar
2 tablespoons inverted sugar, or pale honey
Pinch of salt

For the caramelized sugar (brûlée):

¼ cup sugar
A few drops of lemon juice

To make the crème: Prepare an ice bath and set aside. Put the cream and the milk together in a saucepan and heat gently to about 110°F. Beat together the egg yolks and sugar until pale ribbons form. Add the inverted sugar or honey and the salt, and mix well. Temper the egg yolk mixture by whisking in some of the scalded milk, then add the egg mixture to the saucepan. While constantly stirring, heat the mixture to 185°F and hold it there for 2 minutes. Then plunge the pan into the ice bath and stir the base to reduce the heat quickly.

Once the base is cold, let it rest in the refrigerator a few hours or overnight.

To make the brûlée: Combine the ingredients in a small saucepan. Wash down any sugar crystals on the side of the pan with a damp silicon brush. Bring to a boil, reduce to medium heat, and cook uncovered without stirring until the mixture begins to darken and caramelize. Then swirl the pan until the caramel is an even, dark brown—it should be about the color of a beer bottle. Pour the caramel onto a silicon mat, put another silicon mat on top, and roll it out with a rolling pin to get a nice, thin layer of caramel. Be careful—the

caramel is HOT! Leave it out to cool, then break it up into small bite-size pieces. Place in the freezer.

Transfer the crème mixture (without the caramel) to an ice cream maker and proceed according to manufacturer's instructions. Once the gelato is ready, put it in a freezer-safe container and mix in the brûlée bits.

Enjoy the gelato immediately, or freeze it and eat it within a few days. Remove from the freezer and place in the refrigerator a few minutes before serving to let it soften, but not melt.

PORCHETTA

(SERVES 8–10)

1 pork loin, about 4 pounds

Salt and pepper

5 tablespoons rosemary

25 sage leaves

2 fennel bulbs, shaved

12 cloves garlic, thinly sliced

1 orange, seeds removed, thinly sliced

5 ounces thinly sliced prosciutto di Parma

2 tablespoons extra virgin olive oil

½ cup pork stock

To butterfly the pork: Place meat with the fatty side down. Identify where the ribs originally met the meat; this is the smoothest point of entry. Starting ½ to 1 inch from the meat, along the rib line, make long, shallow cuts to slowly open out and flatten the meat on the board. Rotate the meat and continue to use long, shallow strokes to naturally uncoil the meat and lay it flat on the cutting board.

To make porchetta: Sprinkle meat with salt and pepper, then layer the herbs, fennel, garlic, and oranges on the inside of the pork loin. Slowly roll the loin back up on itself, making sure to keep all of the stuffing in.

To truss the porchetta, lay out 4 parallel pieces of kitchen string cut somewhat longer than the circumference of the loin. Lay a fifth string, considerably more than twice the length of the loin, across the 4 shorter pieces. Place half of the prosciutto on the longer string where it crosses the others. With its open side down, set the rolled loin on top of the prosciutto base and drape with the remaining prosciutto. Tie the loin up lengthwise and then crosswise, cutting off the excess string.

To Cook: Preheat oven to 375°F. Sear the porchetta in olive oil on all sides in a large pan, then place on a roasting rack in a baking dish and add the pork stock. (A thickly sliced onion or fennel may be used in place of the rack to keep the meat out of the stock, but the rack works best.) Bake until the meat reaches an internal temperature of 140°F, approximately 40 minutes. Allow to rest, and slice.

Mostarda

Mostarda is a seemingly uncomplicated recipe but it takes five days of love and attention. It can be made with any seasonal fruit from figs to pumpkins. Fig is the most popular, but I have done blueberry, yellow squash, plum, kumquat, apple, and peach so far. The possibilities are endless.

(MAKES 1-2 QUARTS)

4 pounds fruit chopped in 1-inch pieces (I do figs whole, slice stone fruit in sixths)

2 pounds sugar

¼ cup mustard seeds

¼ cup mustard oil (the American kind, not the coveted senape)

2 tablespoons Dijon mustard

Day 1: Combine the fruit and the sugar and allow to sit at room temperature for 24 hours, covered with cheesecloth.

Days 2, 3: Simply bring the mixture to a boil. Do not boil for longer than a few seconds. Then allow to sit at room temperature, covered with cheesecloth, for 24 hours.

Day 4: Bring to a boil and add mustard seeds. Allow to sit for another 24 hours.

Day 5: Bring to a boil for 5 minutes, adding mustard oil and Dijon at the end for added spice.

Afterwards, can the extras and keep at room temperature for something beautiful and delicious. It's great with almost any cheese or meat as a spread, a sauce, or a condiment.

Note: Room temperature is 73° to 78°F. If you expect it to be much warmer than that, leave the mostarda in a dark cupboard or even in the refrigerator. Allow for 36 hours between steps if you choose to keep it in the fridge.

Pralines by Jean

1728 Saint Charles Avenue
(504) 525-1910
pralinesbyjean.com
Executive Chef: Jean Stickney

On Saint Charles Avenue, smack-dab next to a highly trafficked pub, is this pretty turquoise-painted candy box of a shop. Jean Stickney and her daughter Rachel run front and back of house to turn out the creamiest pralines to ever cross a lip. They make several flavors and sizes of pralines bagged and boxed to go, and they sell fun party knickknacks and New Orleans Saints–inspired cupcakes as well as fanwear such as T-shirts and bead necklaces. The cupcakes are the sleeper of the store, but those in the know come here for the fun flavors—King Cake, Pralines & Cream Cheese, Almond Joy, New Orleans Nectar—just-right-size cupcakes and joie de vivre that bursts from every nook and cranny.

Praline Pumpkin Spice Cupcakes

(MAKES 24 CUPCAKES)

2 cups cake flour

2 teaspoons baking powder

1 teaspoon ground cinnamon

½ teaspoon ground nutmeg

¼ teaspoon ground cloves

½ teaspoon baking soda

½ teaspoon salt

½ cup (1 stick) unsalted butter, at room temperature

1 tablespoon vegetable oil

1½ cups (packed) light brown sugar

2 large eggs

½ cup whole milk

1 cup boiled, mashed pumpkin (may use canned)

½ cup praline debris or crumbled pralines

Preheat oven to 350°F. Line muffin tins with cupcake liners. Sift flour, baking powder, cinnamon, nutmeg, cloves, baking soda, and salt into a medium bowl.

Using electric mixer, beat butter and oil in large bowl until fluffy. Gradually beat in sugar. Beat in eggs one at a time. Beat in flour mixture in thirds alternately with the milk, beginning and ending with flour. Beat in pumpkin. Fold in praline debris. Fill muffin cups with batter using a number-20 scoop (that is, one-twentieth of a quart, or 3.2 tablespoons).

Bake cupcakes until toothpick inserted into center comes out clean, about 22 to 25 minutes. Cool cupcakes in tins on cooling racks for 10 minutes. Remove cupcakes and place on racks. Cool cupcakes completely. Frost with Blood Orange Cream Cheese Frosting.

Blood Orange Cream Cheese Frosting

(MAKES 30 FROSTING SERVINGS)

1 cup (2 sticks) unsalted butter, at room temperature

2 (8-ounce) packages chilled cream cheese

¾ cup (packed) dark brown sugar

1 tablespoon molasses (optional)

1 tablespoon vanilla extract

4 tablespoons blood orange juice

3 cups sifted powdered sugar, plus ¼ cup more as needed

1½ teaspoons grated blood orange peel

30 praline pecan pieces (optional)

Beat butter, cream cheese, brown sugar, molasses, vanilla, and orange juice in large bowl of mixer until fluffy. On a low speed, gradually add sifted powdered sugar and blend until well combined. Turn mixer off. Scrape sides and bottom of bowl. Add orange peel and beat on high speed until well blended and fluffy, but be careful not to overbeat. If frosting becomes too limp, refrigerate entire bowl of frosting with paddle for 10 minutes. Return to mixer and beat on high speed 2 to 3 minutes until fluffy.

Dollop 2 tablespoons onto each cupcake and add a praline piece on top.

Sucré

3025 Magazine Street
(504) 520-8311
shopsucre.com
Executive Chef: Tariq Hanna

The front windows of this "sweets boutique" are always filled with something to gawk at—cakes shaped like pro football helmets, French macarons fashioned into trees, gorgeous fondant-draped wedding cakes, giant papier-mâché ice cream cones . . . This pretty spot is the genius of local catering guru Joel Dondis and brilliant pastry chef/ TV star Tariq Hanna. Marble-topped tables evoke the ice cream parlor feel with style, and the place is always immaculate, bow-tied and precious.

Crystal clear oversized glass cases are filled with ice creams (don't miss the Rocher studded with chunks of the yummy hazelnut-chocolate candy), sorbets, and macarons in fabulous flavors like Blackberry-Lemon or White Chocolate Lavender. Plated desserts, cakes, parfaits, and other stunning pastries sit alongside handmade chocolates, bark, bars, marshmallows, and drinking chocolate. It's all glorious, every single bite.

Banana Beignets with Rum Caramel

(SERVES 8)

3 ripe bananas
Oil for deep frying

For the rum caramel:

1 cup sugar
½ cup brown sugar
¼ cup heavy cream
2 tablespoons butter
1 vanilla bean, scraped
2 tablespoons New Orleans rum

For the dough:

2 cups all-purpose flour
5 eggs
1½ teaspoon salt
2 tablespoons sugar
1 teaspoon instant yeast
3 tablespoons butter
2 tablespoons milk

To make the caramel: Cook sugars until brown and evenly melted. Carefully add cream and butter, then scraped vanilla bean and rum. Stir until smooth. May be served warm or at room temperature.

To make the beignets: Mix all dough ingredients in electric mixer with paddle attachment, about 8 minutes, until smooth and elastic.

Cover bowl and leave dough to rise until doubled in size. Flatten out on floured surface and roll to ⅛-inch thickness.

Cut out 8 pairs of dough disks with a 3-inch cutter. For each pair, fill one disk with a teaspoonful of freshly diced banana. Place the other disk on top and press edges to seal.

Place beignets on a tray and allow to double in size. Fry in oil at 350°F until golden brown, about 1 minute on each side. Allow to cool slightly and serve with rum caramel.

UPTOWN

COMPANY BURGER

4600 FRERET STREET
(504) 267-0320
THECOMPANYBURGER.COM
CHEF: ADAM BIDERMAN

Young and full of "piss and vinegar," Chef Adam Biderman applied skills learned during his time cooking at Atlanta's Holeman & Finch, to return home to New Orleans and open the Company Burger in 2011. He launched his burger joint with a plan to do "the best burger, my way," and that meant no lettuce or tomato. "Nothing's better than good meat, American cheese, and an excellent bun," he preached and preached and preached. Adam stuck to his guns, and the bold move paid off—he routinely sells out. Today diners can get a slice of tomato on their burger, as long as tomatoes are in season. That is Adam's mantra: it has to make sense and be in season to be on the menu—or on the burger. In fact, there are now a lot of seasonal vegetable offerings as salads, or sides to the beef, turkey, or lamb patties. A nearby cocktail emporium, Cure, partners to offer adult beverages, and they're also on hand for special food/cocktail pop-up events that take place on Tuesdays, the day Company is "closed." Company Burger sits on a stretch

of Freret Street that is enjoying a renaissance and reinvigoration of what was once a bustling business district, and Adam is certainly an important and vigorous part of the comeback. Sharing a vegetable side dish was his way of being the smart-ass that he is. He is well loved for just that kind of attitude and a killer burger.

LOCAL CORN & CHERRY TOMATO SALAD

(SERVES 6–8)

8 ears corn, preferably yellow sweet, in the husk

3 pints cherry tomatoes, ideally yellow, red, and black

3 bunches fresh basil, washed and shredded into chiffonade

4 bunches green onion, thinly sliced

3 cloves fresh garlic, minced

3 tablespoons celery seed

2 tablespoons honey

Salt and pepper

2 cups cider vinegar

1½ cups extra virgin olive oil

To prepare the corn: Heat oven to 350°F and cook corn in the husk until your kitchen smells like roasting corn, about 30 to 45 minutes.

Cool the corn and, after 15 minutes, start shucking. The silk will have steamed out of the ears and will come out clean. Brush any remaining hairs off with a towel. Cut the corn off the cob using a sharp knife. Placing the corn in a large bowl or baking dish helps keep all the kernels from flying everywhere. Hold the corncob vertically, applying pressure to the top of the cob so you don't lose it. With a mandoline, this job is significantly easier, but make sure that you have set the opening wide enough to get the whole kernels.

To assemble the salad: Wash the tomatoes and cut them in half. Set aside.

Combine the corn, basil, green onions, garlic, celery seed, and honey, and season lightly with salt and pepper.

Add half of the vinegar and oil and mix. Adjust seasoning to taste (I like heavy pepper). Add remaining vinegar and oil, mix, and toss in tomatoes at the end. Adjust seasoning or vinegar, depending how tart you want it. Ideally the salad should be balanced, like a vinaigrette. Let the salad stand in the refrigerator at least 4 hours before serving. Cold is good, room temperature is better.

CREOLE CREAMERY

4924 PRYTANIA STREET
(504) 894-8680
CREOLECREAMERY.COM
CHEFS/OWNERS: DAVID BERGERON AND BRYAN GILMORE

Tucked inside the former and legendary McKenzie's Bakery building on Prytania Street, David Bergeron and Bryan Gilmore spin artisan ice creams and sorbets, in a traditional American ice cream parlor setting. The best part is the creative flavors that span from Red Velvet, Lavender Honey, or Cucumber Dill to I Scream Fudge!, White Chocolate–Peanut Butter Pie, and many, many more. They do seasonal flavors like Christmas Morning, and every now and then there is homage to McKenzie's Bakery or other food icons like Hubig's Apple Pie. The shop is always buzzing, and they are often featured on the Food Network. This recipe combines the licorice-like flavor of Herbsaint, an anise-flavored liqueur that gives the ice cream its green color, with zesty orange and rich dark chocolate. Very New Orleans.

GREEN FAIRY ICE CREAM

(MAKES ABOUT 2 QUARTS)

¾ cup sugar

5 large egg yolks

3 cups half-and-half

1 cup heavy cream

Pinch of salt

½ cup Herbsaint

¼ teaspoon pure vanilla extract

½ cup dark chocolate (we use Valrhona), chopped

½ cup candied orange peel, cut into ¼-inch cubes

Mix the sugar and egg yolks together in a bowl with a whisk. Meanwhile, heat the half-and-half, cream, and salt in a saucepan. Don't boil it; just heat it to a light simmer. Then pour it slowly into the egg-sugar mixture, whisking as you do it.

Pour it all into the saucepan and cook over low heat, stirring, until it has thickened enough that it will coat the back of a spoon, 8 to 10 minutes. Remove from heat and let cool. Cover with plastic wrap so no skin forms, and put in the refrigerator for a few hours.

When chilled, add Herbsaint and vanilla. Process the mixture in an ice cream maker until frozen to soft-serve consistency, about 20 to 30 minutes. Remove from ice cream maker into a metal or glass container, and fold in the chocolate and orange peel. Cover again with plastic wrap or wax paper, and store in freezer for 6 to 8 hours.

Fat Hen Grill

7457 Saint Charles Avenue
(504) 266-2921
FATHENGRILL.COM
Chef: Shane Pritchett

Chef Shane Pritchett is another well-known New Orleans chef and Emeril's veteran. He began his local career working as executive sous-chef at Emeril's, then in 2004 was made executive chef of Emeril's Delmonico. Shane stayed within the Emeril fold until 2007, when he broke out on his own to open the diner-style Fat Hen. His current iteration of Fat Hen is a grocery and deli on toney Saint Charles Avenue, in the building that was once and famously a Piggly-Wiggly. He and his wife Juliet run what they call a "fine diner" offering over-the-top breakfast dishes (the Womlette is an omelet atop a waffle), lunch plates, and comforting, homey dinners. Shane is also all about serious barbecue, even becoming a certified barbecue judge for the Kansas City Barbecue Society. So no one misses out, the grocery-deli also sells a nice stash of ShaneMade jams, jellies, sauces, baked goods and sweets, smoked meats, and pickles. Coffee geeks too, Shane and Juliet also stock local roasts for their coffee and espresso bar.

Chicken & Dumplings

(SERVES 6)

For the chicken:

1 whole chicken
2 quarts water
1 cup diced onion
1 cup diced celery
1 cup diced carrot
1 teaspoon dried sage
3 teaspoons picked fresh thyme
1 bay leaf
Salt and pepper
6 asparagus spears, blanched, cut into 2-inch pieces
1 ear, yellow corn

For the roux:

¼ pound butter
¾ cup flour

For the dumpling dough:

1½ cups all-purpose flour
2 teaspoons baking powder
¾ teaspoon salt
3 tablespoons shortening
¾ cup milk

To make the chicken: Place chicken in water with diced vegetables and herbs and boil until tender, about 1 hour. Remove chicken from broth, pick off the meat, and discard the bones. Put chicken meat off to the side to cool. Reduce broth to 1 quart, then season to taste with salt and pepper.

To make the roux: In a heavy pan, melt the butter and stir in the flour. Cook over moderate heat, stirring occasionally, until the roux has browned to the color of peanut butter.

Bring broth back up to a boil and add the roux. Whisk and simmer for 20 minutes. Add chicken meat, asparagus, and corn.

To make the dumplings: Preheat oven to 350°F.

Whisk together the flour, baking powder, and salt in a mixing bowl. Cut in the shortening with a knife or pastry blender until the mixture resembles fine crumbs. Stir the milk into the flour mixture until moistened. Dough will be pretty lumpy, but be sure to not over mix it!

Drop dough by large spoonfuls onto the chicken mix in casserole. The dumplings should rest on top of vegetables and meat; it's okay if they stick out of the top a bit. Cook in oven uncovered for 10 minutes, cover and then cook another 10 minutes.

STRAWBERRY RHUBARB FRENCH TOAST

(SERVES 4)

For the rhubarb compote:

2 pounds rhubarb, trimmed and cut in 1-inch pieces

1½ cups sugar

1 tablespoon lemon juice and lemon zest

1 tablespoon orange zest

2 vanilla beans, scraped

1 tablespoon minced ginger

For the Royal Batter:

12 eggs

1 quart half-and-half

4 ounces honey

2 teaspoons cinnamon

For the French toast:

8 (2-inch) slices brioche Pullman loaf

1 quart Royal Batter

¼ pound butter

4 ounces caramel sauce

4 cups sliced fresh strawberries

2 cups rhubarb compote

To make the compote: Combine ingredients and simmer until sugar is dissolved and rhubarb is very tender. Set aside.

To make the Royal Batter: Whisk the eggs in a large basin, then whisk in half-and half, honey, and cinnamon.

To make the French toast: Preheat oven to 350°F.

Soak 2 brioche slices in batter for 45 seconds. Remove from batter and let drain for 1 minute. Bring a pan to medium-high heat and add 2 tablespoons of butter. Add French toast to pan and cook approximately 3 minutes per side, then set aside in a heat-proof baking dish.

Repeat until all French toast is browned in butter.

Bake the French toast in the 350°F oven for approximately 10 minutes until no moisture is left in the middle of the bread. Meanwhile, warm the caramel sauce.

Cut each slice of French toast in half, and shingle four pieces on each of four plates. Divide strawberries and rhubarb on top. Drizzle with caramel sauce.

Gabrielle at the Uptowner

438 Henry Clay Avenue
(504) 899-6500
GABRIELLERESTAURANT.COM
Chefs/Owners: Greg and Mary Sonnier

Executive chefs and owners Greg and Mary Sonnier are a culinary imperative to New Orleans. Their original restaurant on Esplanade in Mid-City was the epicenter for classic-modern Louisiana dishes. Famous for their Slow Roasted Duck atop thin frites (the duck fat juice lusciously coating those fries), and the cool and wonderful Peppermint Patti, Greg and Mary cooked a lot of "firsts" that have inspired a slew of famous local chefs. In 2005 Greg was nominated for a James Beard Award for Best Chef, South, and only a few months later their eponymous restaurant was ruined by the fallout of Hurricane Katrina. Since then they have worked to open a new restaurant, done special dinners, and kept their fans happy as best they can. Because they love New Orleans, Greg and Mary shared recipes for two of their very popular dishes. Lucky us!

JJ's Lemon Chess Pie
(SERVES 8)

For the cornmeal pie crust:

1 cup all-purpose flour
¼ cup yellow cornmeal
½ teaspoon salt
2 teaspoons sugar
4 ounces cold butter
¼ cup cold milk

For the pie filling:

2 cups granulated sugar
4 ounces unsalted butter, softened
1 tablespoon all-purpose flour
2 tablespoons cornmeal
Dash of salt
4 large eggs, at room temperature
¼ cup half-and-half, at room temperature
¼ cup lemon juice, freshly squeezed
2 teaspoons grated lemon rind

To make the crust: Mix together all dry ingredients. Working quickly, cut the butter in until it is pea size. Sprinkle milk on top and work mixture with your fingers, just until it sticks together. Form into a patty, wrap well in film, and allow to rest in refrigerator for 1 hour.

Roll dough out and place in a 9-inch pie pan. Put into the freezer for 20 minutes. Preheat oven to 375°F.

To blind-bake the pie crust, line it with a piece of parchment paper, fill with pie weights (dried beans work well, or rice), and put into hot oven. After 15 minutes, remove parchment and weights. Put crust back into oven, reducing heat to 325°F; bake another 15 minutes or until set and blond.

Remove pie crust and lower oven setting to 300°F.

To make the filling: Place sugar in a food processor and process until superfine. Add butter and process until creamy. Beat in flour, cornmeal, and salt. Add eggs, one at a time, and beat well after each addition. Beat in half-and-half, lemon juice, and rind.

Pour mixture into blind-baked 9-inch cornmeal pie shell and bake (on low shelf) in 300°F oven for 50 to 60 minutes. Cool thoroughly before cutting.

FUSILLI WITH SHRIMP & CRACKER-CRUSTED RABBIT

(SERVES 6–8)

2 eggs

2 cups unsalted cracker crumbs

⅓ cup chopped fresh parsley

¾ teaspoon salt

½ teaspoon freshly ground black pepper

½ pound boneless rabbit tenderloin (or chicken tenders)

4 tablespoons extra virgin olive oil

½ pound large shrimp, peeled and deveined

⅔ cup dry white wine

1 cup whipping cream

¼ teaspoon cayenne pepper

¼ cup freshly grated Parmesan

½ pound fusilli pasta

2 tablespoons chopped fresh basil

Crack the eggs into a shallow bowl and whisk to blend. In a separate shallow bowl, mix together the cracker crumbs, parsley, salt, and black pepper. Dip the rabbit first into the eggs and then into the cracker mixture. Be sure to coat completely.

Heat 3 tablespoons of the olive oil in a heavy, large skillet over medium-high heat. Add the rabbit and sauté until it is cooked through, about 4 minutes per side. Transfer the rabbit to a plate and discard the oil in the skillet.

Add 1 tablespoon of olive oil to the hot skillet, add shrimp, and sauté over medium heat until just cooked through, about 2 minutes. Use a slotted spoon to transfer the shrimp to the plate of rabbit.

Now add the white wine to the skillet and boil until reduced to ½ cup, about 2 minutes. Add the whipping cream and simmer until the sauce thickens slightly, about 3 minutes. Stir in the cayenne pepper and the Parmesan cheese.

Cut the rabbit into pieces and put both the rabbit and the shrimp, as well as any collected juices, in the skillet with the sauce. Stir over medium heat until all is heated thoroughly. Meanwhile, cook the fusilli in a large pot of boiling, salted water until just tender.

Drain the pasta and add it to the skillet. Toss to coat the pasta, and season with salt and pepper. Transfer to a large serving bowl; sprinkle with the basil and serve.

High Hat

4500 Freret Street
(504) 754.1336
highhatcafe.com
Chef: Jeremy Wolgamott
Owner: Adolfo Garcia

Chef Adolfo Garcia is a very well-liked chef in New Orleans. His culinary prowess goes way back, but he is best known for opening RioMar (seafood), then La Boca (meat-centric), A Mano (rustic Italian), and most recently Ancora (Neapolitan-style pizza) and High Hat (southern inspired). He and his restaurants are quite the tour de force. With his business partner Chip Apperson and Chef Jeremy Wolgamott in the kitchen, all three guys showcase mad love for southern food, and the menu fairly is ring-the-dinner-bell! delicious. Their tag line, "The Delta comes to the Bayou," says it all.

Stewed Chicken with Mustard Greens & Spoon Bread

Stewed chicken is a classic southern dish that can be found cooking on the stove at Grandma's house on any Sunday afternoon. It is usually pretty heavy, and an after-lunch nap is almost required. This version is made lighter with the addition of lemon juice and fresh herbs. To help cut through some of the richness, it is best served with vinegary braised greens and spoon bread. The greens help to round out the dish without making you sleepy, and the spoon bread soaks up the delicious gravy dripping off the chicken without being as filling as a traditional bread or steamed rice.

(SERVES 4)

For the chicken:

1 chicken, quartered, backbone removed
Salt and pepper
Soybean oil, up to ½ cup
½ cup flour
⅔ cup diced yellow onion
⅓ cup diced celery
⅓ cup diced bell pepper
3 cloves garlic, minced
½ teaspoon cayenne pepper
1 quart chicken stock
1 bunch fresh thyme
1 tablespoon sliced green onions
1 tablespoon chopped parsley
1 teaspoon hot sauce, or to taste
½ teaspoon lemon juice, or to taste

For the mustard greens:

2 yellow onions, sliced
1 tablespoon chopped garlic
½ cup bacon pieces
1 ham hock
¼ cup light brown sugar
½ teaspoon crushed red pepper
1 pint Abita amber beer
4 tablespoons red wine vinegar, divided
1 pint chicken stock

5 bunches mustard greens, chopped
Salt and pepper to taste

For the spoon bread:

1 quart whole milk
¾ cup coarse yellow cornmeal
¼ cup yellow corn flour
2 tablespoons unsalted butter
1½ teaspoons salt
4 egg yolks
4 egg whites

To make the chicken: Season chicken pieces with salt and pepper. Heat a large cast iron pan over medium-high heat and coat with oil. Cook chicken, skin side down, in batches until the skin is turning brown and crispy. Set chicken aside.

Pour oil and chicken fat from pan into a measuring container and add enough oil to make ½ cup. Return oil to pan and heat until almost smoking. Whisk in flour and cook over medium heat, stirring constantly, until the roux turns the color of milk chocolate. Turn off the heat and add onions, celery, bell pepper, garlic, and cayenne. Stir until well mixed. Set aside.

In a large pot bring chicken stock to a boil. Carefully mix in the roux and whisk until incorporated.

Turn down heat and simmer for ten minutes, skimming any fat that rises to the surface.

Preheat oven to 350°F. Place chicken pieces in a roasting pan. Tie fresh thyme with butcher's twine and add to pan. Pour in enough of the thickened stock to cover everything. Cover roasting pan with parchment paper and foil, then place in oven for 3 hours, or until the chicken reaches an internal temperature of 175°F. Remove from oven and uncover. Let the chicken cool in the liquid for at least 3 hours or overnight.

Remove the chicken from the braising liquid and set aside. Put all of the liquid into a large pot and reduce by one-third, skimming any fat that rises. Transfer to a smaller pot and keep warm on the stove.

To make the mustard greens: In a large pot, sweat onions, garlic, bacon, and ham hocks. Add brown sugar and red pepper and cook until sugar is starting to caramelize. Pour in beer, 2 tablespoons vinegar, and stock and bring to a boil. Add greens and cook until tender, then season with salt, pepper, and the remaining 2 tablespoons vinegar.

To make the spoon bread: Preheat oven to 400°F. Grease a 9 x 9-inch baking pan.

Bring the milk up to a boil and whisk in the cornmeal and corn flour. Cook over medium-high heat for about 5 minutes, stirring constantly. Add the butter and salt and remove from the heat. Whisk in the egg yolks one at a time. Beat the egg whites until they hold medium peaks, and fold them into the hot batter. Pour into the greased baking pan and bake uncovered for 30 to 45 minutes. It should rise considerably and be golden brown on top, but will not seem set. Remove from the oven and let stand in a warm area for 10 minutes to firm up, and then serve immediately.

To finish the dish: Heat a 12-inch skillet and add the cooked chicken, skin side down. Cover with the braising liquid and bring to a boil. Turn down to a simmer, cover, and cook until the chicken is warmed through and starting to fall off the bone. Carefully remove and set one chicken quarter on each of four serving plates. To the sauce add the green onions, parsley, hot sauce, and lemon juice, and taste for seasoning. Spoon sauce over chicken and serve with a large spoonful of mustard greens and a large spoonful of spoon bread.

BLUEBERRY CANE SYRUP PIE IN A CORNMEAL CRUST

(SERVES 8)

For the crust:

2¼ cups all-purpose flour
½ cup coarse yellow cornmeal
2 tablespoons sugar
1 teaspoon kosher salt
½ stick unsalted butter
½ cup lard
½ cup buttermilk

For the filling:

4½ cups fresh blueberries
⅓ cup cane syrup
3 tablespoon sugar
7 teaspoons cornstarch
5 teaspoons lemon juice
Pinch of ground cinnamon

Put the dry ingredients for the crust into a food processor. Pulse six times. Scatter the butter and lard over dry mix and pulse ten times. Slowly pour in buttermilk while pulsing twelve more times.

Move dough to a mixing bowl and knead a few times until a ball forms. Separate into two-thirds and one-third, and form into disks. Wrap disks separately and place in refrigerator for at least 15 minutes, or overnight.

Remove larger disk from fridge and let sit at room temperature for 15 minutes.

Roll out large disk, fit it into a 10-inch pie pan, and place back in fridge.

Preheat oven to 400°F. Remove smaller dough disk from fridge and let sit for 15 minutes. Meanwhile, mix filling ingredients in a large bowl and let sit for 10 minutes. Pour filling into chilled pie shell.

Roll out smaller crust until large enough to cover pie. Using your fingers, dab outside rim of bottom crust with water and cover with top crust, pressing together with a fork to seal. Trim the excess crust off with a small knife and cut vents into the top crust. Bake at 400°F for 30 minutes. Rotate the pie and bake for another 30 minutes at 350°F, or until juice is slowly bubbling through the vent holes.

Remove from oven and let cool for 2 hours before serving. Serve warm with fresh whipped cream and peach ice cream.

LA PETITE GROCERY

4238 MAGAZINE STREET
(504) 891-3377
LAPETITEGROCERY.COM
CHEF/OWNER: JUSTIN DEVILLIER
CO-OWNER: MIA FREIBERGER-DEVILLIER

Justin Devillier, executive chef since 2007, and Mia, manager since 2009, took over ownership of this comfortably stylish restaurant two years ago, infusing it with Chef Justin's love for unique ingredients, locally sourced and sometimes even hand grown. The menu has a bistro vibration and the food is both smart and sexy. There is a bar area with seating for those who want a properly made cocktail and a bite, or you can step into the main dining room for the full experience. Sunday brunch is soothing, and the outdoor seating is great for watching Magazine Street's bustle. Some pop in to La Petite Grocery for the sweets of pastry chef Bronwen Wyatt, coffee, or champagne.

Tagliatelle with Gulf Shrimp & Field Peas

Chef Justin loves local seafood and he loves making pasta. Both are incredible when combined with the earthiness of field peas and heady aged Parmesan.

(SERVES 4)

2 tablespoons salt

1 pound fresh Gulf shrimp, preferably 12-count

½ cup cooked black-eyed peas

½ cup cooked soybeans

5 ounces salt, divided 1 ounce and 4 ounces

12 ounces fresh tagliatelle

2 ounces unsalted butter

Salt to taste

1 teaspoon white pepper

2 tablespoons snipped chives

2 ounces lemon juice

1 tablespoon picked oregano

8 grams shaved Piave vecchio or aged Parmesan

Fill a large pot with 8 to 10 quarts of water, add 2 tablespoons salt, and bring to a boil. Meanwhile, place ¼ cup water in a large saucepan and bring to a simmer. Add the shrimp and gently cook through. Add the peas and beans to warm.

To the large pot of water add the pasta and cook until al dente, about 5 to 10 minutes, tasting frequently after the first 2 minutes. Drain and keep warm.

In the pan with the shrimp, peas, and beans, gently swirl in the butter over low heat. Place the pasta in the pan with the shrimp-peas-butter sauce and season with salt to taste, pepper, chives, and lemon juice. Serve garnished with oregano and shaved cheese.

BUTTERSCOTCH PUDDING

Pastry chef Bronwen Wyatt first encountered an upscale butterscotch pudding while working with James Beard–nominated pastry chef Michelle Polzine in San Francisco. Her version returns the dessert to its southern roots, incorporating Louisiana cane syrup and New Orleans rum, and serves it with toasted pecan madeleines.

(SERVES 6–8)

3 ounces butter

1 tablespoon Steen's cane syrup or molasses

½ pound dark brown sugar

3 tablespoons amber or dark rum

½ teaspoon salt, or more to taste

4¼ cups cream

1 vanilla bean

¾ cup plus 2 tablespoons granulated sugar

3 sheets gelatin or 1 tablespoon gelatin powder

6 egg yolks

Special equipment: **pastry brush**

Melt butter with cane syrup. Add brown sugar, rum, and salt and cook over medium heat until bubbling and just beginning to smoke. Add 4 cups cream and whisk until caramel is dissolved. Scrape seeds out of vanilla bean and add both seeds and bean to cream mixture. Cover and allow to steep.

Meanwhile, combine granulated sugar and ¼ cup water in a heavy-bottomed, nonreactive pot. Cover and bring to a boil. When steam begins to escape, remove the lid. Allow sugar to caramelize to a deep amber, brushing down sides of pot frequently to prevent crystallization. Once caramel is ready, immediately take it off the heat and whisk in the remaining ¼ cup cream. Add this caramel mixture to cream mixture, whisk thoroughly, and gently warm until caramel is totally dissolved.

At this point, begin to bloom gelatin by submerging sheets in ice water (if using powdered gelatin, follow manufacturer's instructions). Then temper some of the warm caramel-cream mixture into the yolks, return yolk mix to the pot, and cook until the pudding is the texture of a thick crème anglaise. Immediately whisk in bloomed gelatin and strain mixture into a bowl set over ice. Allow to cool until moderately thickened before portioning into small, wide-mouthed mason jars or other decorative containers. Allow to set for at least 4 hours.

Serve with gently whipped cream and cookies.

Martinique

5908 Magazine Street
(504) 891-8495
MARTINIQUEBISTRO.COM
Owners: Cristiano Raffignone & Kelly Barker
Executive Chef: Eric LaBouchere

Owners Cristiano Raffignone and Kelly Barker first dined here in the 1990s, and they loved it so much they bought the place in 2003. Since then, they've lovingly remodeled the building and enhanced the outdoor dining patio with lush foliage to turn it into a popular, utterly lovely dining courtyard that is particularly romantic in the cool of an evening. Executive Chef Eric LaBouchere and Sous-Chef Nat Carrier are thoughtful and wise, putting an eclectic spin on the French/Mediterranean cuisine. This restaurant oozes upscale casual, fine dining charm and sophistication.

CRAWFISH BOIL GNOCCHI

SWEET CORN GNOCCHI A LA PARISIENNE WITH CREMINI MUSHROOMS, SMOKED TASSO, ROASTED GARLIC, CELERY HEART & LOUISIANA CRAWFISH TAILS

There is a lot of local love for the pillowy Parisienne gnocchi at Martinique. This Louisiana-inspired preparation is a standout and a serious crowd pleaser. Chef Nat says, "While the making of the dough and the blanching of the gnocchi are a bit time consuming, the reaction you and others will experience on first bite will be worth the effort."

(SERVES 6)

For the pâte à choux:

2 cups water

6 ounces unsalted butter, cut in small cubes

1 teaspoon crab boil spice

5 ounces all-purpose flour, sifted

5 ounces corn flour (available in specialty market), sifted

8 eggs

For the boil:

Boil seasonings to personal taste (see note 1)

3 cups heavy cream

For the gnocchi sauté:

8 ounces unsalted butter, cubed

1 pound cremini mushrooms, cleaned and quartered

2 cups corn kernels (about 10 ears), lightly roasted

2 whole heads of garlic, roasted

¼ pound tasso, thinly sliced (see note 2)

1 pound of bagged frozen crawfish tails, thawed

1 bunch green onions, cleaned and thinly sliced

3 cups gnocchi sauce base

Celery heart leaves from 1 bunch celery

Note 1: To season a 2-gallon boil, you will want to use a pre-made boiling spice such as Zatarain's or other store-bought seafood boil seasoning mix and 2 whole onions, 1 bunch celery, trimmed, and 2 lemons and 2 oranges, halved.

Note 2: Tasso, a Cajun/Creole specialty, is a shoulder ham that is brined, then heavily spiced and cold-smoked. We cure and smoke our own. Poche's is an excellent tasso. If unavailable outside Louisiana, the nearest equivalent might be serrano ham or other good quality smoked ham.

To make the pâte à choux: Combine water, butter, and boil spice in a wide, heavy-bottomed sauce pot and bring to a simmer over low heat. When butter is completely dissolved, slowly add sifted flours, continually folding to incorporate with a wooden spoon. Once all flour is in and dough begins to pull away from sides of pot, remove from heat. Continue folding until dough has formed into a semi-firm ball. Add eggs 2 at a time, folding until dough tightens back up between additions. Transfer part of the dough to a piping bag fitted with a ½-inch to ¾-inch cylindrical tip (you will have to reload throughout the cooking process). Cover remaining dough with plastic film and place piping bag and dough in a cold corner to rest for 20 minutes while you prepare your boil.

To make the boil: In a large pot, place 2 gallons of water along with desired seafood boil seasonings and bring to a boil over high heat. Remember to properly adjust salt and spice first, and then add citrus only to steep, so as to prevent bitterness. Once the boil liquid has full flavor, strain through a fine mesh sieve and return to a simmer.

Prepare an ice bath. You will also need a sharp paring knife and a spider (metal strainer spoon) to remove the gnocchi once blanched.

Working in small batches, pipe the gnocchi dough into the simmering pot, using the paring knife to cut the dough into even ½-inch cylinders. Once the gnocchi float to the surface and begin to expand, remove with spider and transfer to ice bath. Repeat until all gnocchi have been blanched.

In a separate pot reduce heavy cream by half. Combine with 2 cups of blanching liquid, and strain through a fine mesh sieve. This is your sauce base.

To make the sauté: Place a large sauté pan, or two, over high heat, with a healthy knob of butter. As the butter foams, add proportional amounts of mushrooms and gnocchi, without overcrowding the pan. Allow the gnocchi and mushrooms to lightly caramelize all over. Remove excess grease, lower heat to medium, add appropriate proportions of corn, garlic, tasso, crawfish, green onions, and sauce base, and return to a steady simmer. Taste one of the gnocchi to check seasoning, adjust as needed, and transfer to warmed serving dish. Garnish with celery heart leaves and serve immediately.

Café Brûlot Ice Cream

Café brûlot is an old-school New Orleans coffee drink made with cognac and aromatic spices, studded into an orange peel. The cognac is flamed tableside and drizzled down the spice-specked orange peel curl into a bowl of hot coffee. This ice cream interpretation is full of classic holiday flavors. It can be made as is, or feel free to increase or decrease quantities of any of the aromatic ingredients, or sugar, to taste.

(SERVES 6–8)

1 whole cinnamon stick, about 5 inches
1 teaspoon whole cloves, toasted
1 quart heavy cream
⅔ cup whole milk
¾ cup New Orleans ground coffee
1 teaspoon vanilla extract
1 vanilla bean
3 satsumas (or oranges, tangerines, or clementines)
¼ cup cognac
11 egg yolks
½ cup sugar

In a large heavy-bottomed sauce pot, lightly toast cinnamon stick and whole cloves over low heat just until you smell their essential oils. Remove cinnamon stick and, once cool enough to handle, break into pieces and return to pot along with heavy cream, milk, ground coffee, vanilla extract, and vanilla bean. (Be sure to split and scrape bean first. Both go into the pot.) Carefully bring the brûlot mixture to a full simmer over low heat, stirring occasionally; the cream wants to boil over; believe us from experience. Once it is up to a simmer, remove from heat. With a vegetable peeler, peel strips of satsuma zest into pot, then juice the citrus and add juice to pot as well. Cool the mixture, transfer to a storage container, and allow to steep for 2 full days. This will allow the aromatics, specifically the coffee and satsuma, to bloom properly.

Return the brûlot mixture to a large heavy-bottomed pot and bring to a simmer over low heat. Using a thermometer, take the cream mixture to 168°F, remove from heat, and stir in the cognac. Place the egg yolks and sugar in the bowl of a stand mixer with whisk attachment. Whisk to combine, scrape any sugar stuck to sides with a rubber spatula, and whip at low speed until pale yellow ribbons form (low speed is to avoid incorporating unwanted air). Strain brûlot mixture through a fine mesh sieve into a suitable container. On low speed, temper by slowly pouring brûlot mixture into egg yolks and sugar. Once completely combined, transfer to storage container to cool under refrigeration overnight. Café brûlot ice cream is ready to be run in an ice cream maker and frozen.

Patois

6078 Laurel Street
(504) 895-9441
PATOISNOLA.COM
Chef/Owner: Aaron Burgau; Co-Owners: Leon and Pierre
Touzet; Pastry Chef: Lisa Gustafson

Tucked away in a predominantly residential neighborhood near Audubon Park, Chef Aaron Burgau and business partners Leon and Pierre Touzet have created a chic French restaurant with a New Orleans accent. Often highly visible at the farmers markets, Chef Aaron is a big supporter of local community gardens and ingredients from nearby farms. The menu changes weekly to reflect what's available, and there is always something fun and different to try on the menu. Patois's pastry is the handiwork of Lisa Gustafson, who takes her cues from relevant flavors of the moment and seasonal fruits. There is also a clever cocktail program created by head bartender Becky Tarpy. Her cocktails are fresh and lively, classic in foundation, and tweaked to be current. Chef Aaron sums it up: "This is a fun place to dine and drink."

LAMB RIBS

(SERVES 2–4 AS APPETIZER)

For the lamb rib rub:

4 tablespoons cumin seed
4 tablespoons fennel seed
4 tablespoons coriander seed
1 cup granulated onion
1 cup granulated garlic
2 teaspoons cayenne
4 tablespoons smoked paprika
2 cups raw sugar
1 cup black pepper
2 cups salt
4 teaspoons allspice
4 teaspoons dry mustard

For the lamb:

1 rack lamb ribs (6–8 ribs)
4 tablespoons lamb rib rub

For the green tomato jam:

5 pounds green tomatoes, diced
2 cups apple cider vinegar
2 cups sugar
2 tablespoons salt
2 tablespoons pickling spice
1 cup onion, diced
1 teaspoon crushed red pepper
2 cloves
½ cinnamon stick

To make the rub: In a nonstick pan, toast cumin, fennel, and coriander seeds. Grind in a spice grinder or mortar and pestle. Combine remaining ingredients and set aside or store in an airtight container until ready to use.

To cook the lamb: Rub lamb ribs with the lamb rib rub. On an outdoor grill/smoker or in a home oven, set temperature to 225°F and cook ribs for about 4 hours, until meat is tender and almost falls off the bones.

To make the jam: In a large stockpot, combine all ingredients and cook for 30 to 40 minutes or until thick.

To plate: When ribs are finished cooking, let them rest, covered lightly, for 10 to 15 minutes, then cut the rack into individual ribs. On a serving plank, place three sets of two ribs stacked crisscross and topped with a generous tablespoon or two of green tomato jam. Serve immediately.

CREOLE CREAM CHEESE SEMIFREDDO

(SERVES 12–15)

12 ounces cream

12 ounces Creole cream cheese

4 yolks

7 ounces sugar, divided

4 egg whites

Whip cream to medium peaks. Run Creole cream cheese through a blender until smooth; fold into whipped cream. Whip yolks and 3 ounces sugar until thick and pale; fold into dairy mixture. Whip egg whites with remaining 4 ounces sugar to form medium-stiff peaks; fold into dairy-yolk mixture. Scoop into fleximold, and smooth the surface. Freeze about 4 hours, or until firm. Unmold and serve.

BLUEBERRY COMPOTE

(MAKES SLIGHTLY MORE THAN 1 PINT)

1½ heaping quarts fresh or frozen blueberries

1½ ounces sugar

2 tablespoons lemon juice

2 (3-inch) cinnamon sticks

Combine all ingredients. Boil for 7 to 8 minutes, or until berries begin to pop. Cool to room temperature to serve.

LEMON–POPPY SEED SHORTBREAD

(MAKES 2 DOZEN)

8 ounces softened butter

Zest of 2 lemons

½ teaspoon lemon oil

½ cup sugar

2 cups all-purpose flour

1 tablespoon poppy seeds

Cream butter, lemon zest, lemon oil, and sugar. Slowly add flour until combined. Stir in poppy seeds.

Roll into logs and refrigerate until firm.

Preheat oven to 350°F. Slice dough logs into ¼-inch slices and place on ungreased cookie sheets. Bake for 10 minutes, turning cookie sheets halfway through baking. Cool shortbread on sheets for five minutes, then on wire racks.

St. James Cheese Company

5004 Prytania Street
(504) 899-4737
STJAMESCHEESE.COM
Owners: Richard and Danielle Sutton

Step through the front door of this petite cheese shop and breathe deep. The heavenly scents of washed rinds, fresh and aging cheeses blend gorgeously with cured meats, yeasty breads, olives, and other condiments. Richard and Danielle Sutton run the show here and were among those who opened soon after the storm, in 2006. Their pedigree in cheesemongering is impeccable, and their love for the city unwavering. They offer cheese classes, hold interesting pairing events (Cocktails and Curds), support local vendors and purveyors, and in short have become essential. Almost every restaurant of note seeks their advice and buys the cheeses they source. Richard and Danielle also offer a wide menu of hot and cold sandwiches, salads, cheese and meat boards—and then there is the obvious, a rich, melty mac and cheese, which they've shared here.

PEPATO MACARONI & CHEESE

This is a very easy and fast mac and cheese recipe, but it also has a lot of complexity. If you can't find pecorino pepato, substitute another pecorino and use a generous amount of freshly ground black pepper.

(SERVES 4–6)

1 stick unsalted butter
½ cup flour
1 large shallot, finely diced
¾ cup white wine
3 cups whole milk
3 cups grated pecorino pepato
1 pound cooked macaroni

Melt butter over medium heat. Whisk in flour and stir for 2 minutes until it smells nutty. Add diced shallots and cook for 1 minute. Whisk in white wine and stir until mixture is smooth. Slowly pour in milk while whisking to make a smooth sauce. Add grated cheese, a bit at a time, and stir until it is completely melted. If the sauce is too thick, you can thin it with a little more milk. You can mix this right away with hot cooked pasta, or refrigerate the sauce for later. It heats up and melts really well on the stovetop or in the microwave.

Alabama Peach Chutney

This chutney is delicious served with cheese or cold meats, on sandwiches, or used as a glaze on a pork roast. It is a great way to avoid throwing out overripe peaches, from a rash moment at the farmers market when you spied them piled beautifully on the table and bought way too many.

(MAKES 4 LARGE OR 8 SMALL JARS)

30 ripe peaches
5 cups cider vinegar
5 cups sugar
3 teaspoons salt
3 white onions, finely chopped
3 cloves garlic, finely chopped
2 tablespoons mustard seeds
2 cups golden raisins

Blanch peaches in boiling water for 3 minutes. Remove and let cool. Peel the peaches and cut fruit away from the pit, chopping it roughly in large chunks.

Combine cider vinegar, sugar, and salt in a large pot and bring to a boil. Add onions and garlic and cook for 5 minutes. Add peaches, mustard seeds, and raisins to the pot and boil for 30 minutes. Reduce heat and simmer for 2 hours.

Prepare and sterilize canning jars. Bring the chutney back up to a boil before removing from heat. Ladle into sterilized jars and add rings and lids. The heat from the chutney will seal the jars. Set on a wire rack to cool.

Taceaux Loceaux

@TLNola

Executive Chefs: Maribeth and Alex Del Castillo

Chef-owners of the first New Orleans food truck of the "gourmet" kind. Taceaux Loceaux rocked their business with cleverly named, superdelicious "taceaux" like Messin' with Texas (slow-roasted brisket, shredded cabbage, radish, cilantro, crema, and salsa on flour tortillas) or Jane Deaux (seasoned braised greens, potatoes, Cotija cheese, crema, salsa, cilantro, and toasted pepitas on corn tortillas). They post on Facebook, use Twitter to update their location and menus, and help spearhead New Orleans's burgeoning food truck movement. Every now and again, Taceaux Loceaux will serve a tricked-out hot dog, a spicy Gulf shrimp taceau, soups, or other specials. The recipe here is just such a "special," one of the fun and tasty surprises that might wind up on their blackboard menu.

Gulf Ceviche

We love this recipe, as it really showcases the beautiful fish from the Gulf Coast. Amberjack, mahi mahi, and snapper are all excellent choices, as is shrimp if you prefer, but defer to your fishmonger's recommendations should those be unavailable in your area. You want the freshest fish you can find.

(SERVES 4)

For the ceviche:

1 pound firm-fleshed fish
Juice of 6 lemons
Juice of 6 limes
¼ cup apple cider vinegar
3 jalapeños, seeds removed, finely minced
5 garlic cloves, finely minced
1 bunch cilantro, chopped
2 teaspoons salt

For the charred jalapeño dressing:

2 jalapeños
3 cloves garlic
½ bunch cilantro, roughly chopped
½ cup sour cream
½ cup mayonnaise
2 tablespoons cider vinegar
Salt to taste

For assembly:

3 corn tortillas
Peanut oil, for frying
Salt
1 head butter lettuce or 8 corn tortillas
2 avocados
½ bunch cilantro, leaves only, for garnish

To make the ceviche: Cut the fish into uniform ½-inch dice. Combine with remaining seven ingredients in a large mixing bowl. Allow to marinate in refrigerator for at least 6 hours and preferably overnight, stirring occasionally.

To make the dressing: Roast jalapeños in oven until skin is blistered and charred. Cool. Remove skin and seeds. Combine all dressing ingredients in blender, and process until smooth. Refrigerate until ready to use.

To assemble: Julienne the 3 tortillas. Heat oil in a heavy-bottomed pot until thermometer registers between 350° and 365°F. Fry tortilla threads until crisp. Salt immediately after removing from oil.

Arrange 3 butter lettuce leaves or 2 corn tortillas on each of four plates. Slice the avocados and add 3 slices to each leaf. Portion ceviche onto each leaf, topping with 1 tablespoon jalapeño dressing. Garnish with fried tortilla threads and cilantro leaves.

In late 2008 I was spending a lot of time at a restaurant called Fuel (now Surrey's) where my friend Maribeth Del Castillo was the chef and where I could feast on her maple-bacon scones. When it was slow enough for her to sit and chat with me for a moment, she talked about how she and her husband were buying a food truck from someone in Florida. Not long thereafter, her husband Alex drove that truck to New Orleans, and not long after that, Taceaux Loceaux was born.

Navigating New Orleans's city laws for food trucks was daunting, frustrating, and time consuming. Ultimately Maribeth and Alex got the permits required, and, leveraging social media for advertising, they got people eating and talking about their "taceaux." They also brought back a style of dining that Hurricane Katrina had all but washed away—they were open late at night. Chefs and restaurant industry folks loved to hit the truck after service, and as word spread, their menu and locations grew. Taceaux Loceaux also served as the impetus for other would-be food truck owners to look into this type of food service.

Interestingly, the truck scene really blossomed in Baton Rouge, where there is a robust truck scene that seems to have started with Nick Hufft and his insanely delicious burger truck Curbside. Both Alex and Nick are the front men for coalitions (New Orleans and Baton Rouge, respectively) seeking to expand mobile food laws, and they are making headway. But it is not without controversy. Currently the number of licenses for mobile food vendors in Orleans Parish is limited, but those that have permits are doing beautifully.

Evidence these food trucks, each with its own delicious food interpretations, crafted by creative cooks on a mission:

- Taceaux Loceaux—Creative "taceauxs" both carnivore and vegetarian
- Brigade Coffee Truck—Espresso, iced coffee, hot coffee
- The French Truck—Micro Coffee Roaster
- La Cocinita—South American food
- Foodie Call—Ramped-up comfort food
- Empanada Intifada—Hand pies
- Rue Chow—American and Louisiana home cooking
- Miss Linda/The Yakamein Lady—East-meets-West noodle soup
- The Fry Bar—Decked-out french fries covered in herbs and served with dipping sauces
- SliderShak—Meat and veg sliders, shakes, frites. More to come . . . believe it!

Tartine

7217 Perrier Street
(504) 866-4860
TARTINENEWORLEANS.COM
Chef/Owner: Cara Benson

Chef-owner Cara Benson is a local gal with a dream and mission: to have "a little piece of Paris in the Black Pearl." Done and done. Nestled into a onetime frame shop abutting "Uptown Square" (the home of the Tuesday Crescent City Farmers Market), Cara and her team, including her husband Evan, bake crisp-crusted baguettes, chewy loaves of ciabatta, tender focaccia, and hearty wheat bread to hold slices of deli meats, creamy cheese, or the house special, slabs of rustic country pâté, pickles, and house-made jams. The scones, brioche, and bagels are also lovely, and there is no skipping the airy yet rich and chocolaty mousse. Always keen to support local businesses, Cara buys much of her produce from the farmers market outside her door, to turn into soups or sandwich fillings. She was among the first to serve and sell locally roasted French Truck Coffees.

Duck Liver Mousse with Peach-Jalapeño Marmalade

(SERVES 10–12)

For the duck liver mousse:

1 pound duck livers (or chicken livers)
1 pound butter, at room temperature
2 shallots, finely diced
1 teaspoon chopped thyme
1 tablespoon salt
¼ teaspoon white pepper
⅛ teaspoon freshly ground nutmeg
⅛ teaspoon ground cloves
¼ cup cognac or other brandy

For the peach-jalapeño marmalade:

1 shallot, finely diced
2 jalapeños, seeds and pith removed, finely diced
1–3 tablespoons olive oil
4 peaches, peeled and diced
¼ cup sugar
2 tablespoons white balsamic vinegar
Salt and pepper, to taste

To make the mousse: Clean, wash, and dry duck livers.

Melt 2 tablespoons butter in a heavy sauté pan over medium-low heat. Sauté diced shallots and thyme until translucent, about 8 minutes. Add duck livers, salt, pepper, nutmeg, and cloves to the pan and cook, turning once, until livers have firmed and are pink on the inside, about 3 to 4 minutes. Remove duck livers and deglaze pan with cognac, then reduce liquid by half and remove from heat.

Transfer livers and liquid to food processor and puree until smooth and slightly cooled. With the machine running, add remaining softened butter a tablespoon at a time to form the mousse.

For the smoothest texture, press the mousse through a mesh sieve using a plastic spatula or a dough scraper.

Transfer finished mousse to an airtight container and cover surface with plastic wrap until ready to use.

To make the marmalade: Sauté shallots and jalapeños in olive oil. Add peaches. Season with sugar, vinegar, salt, and pepper. Bring mixture to a boil, reduce heat to a simmer, and cook until thickened.

Dark Chocolate Mousse

(SERVES 6–8)

18 ounces dark chocolate
1 quart cream
9 egg yolks
1 egg
7 ounces sugar

Melt chocolate and keep warm. Whip cream to soft peaks. Beat yolks and egg. Cook sugar with enough water to cover until it reaches soft-ball stage (234°F). Stream sugar syrup into eggs while whipping on high. When ribbon stage is reached, fold into whipped cream. Fold in warm melted chocolate.

Transfer mousse to a serving bowl or to individual serving cups. Chill at least 2 to 3 hours before serving.

CARROLLTON & RIVERBEND

Cowbell

8801 Oak Street
(504) 298-8689
COWBELL-NOLA.COM
Executive Chef: Brack May

Chef Brack May began his New Orleans restaurant life at a cool place in the Central Business District called Cobalt. He was an innovator and the guy who introduced New Orleans diners to Chicken & Waffles, his way—crispy fried chicken with brown gravy and Steen's cane syrup, mashed potatoes on the side. His style tends toward eclectic modern, and he is always animated and a ton of fun. Cobalt closed, but Brack stayed around the city and lent his considerable skills to a number of restaurant/food-related projects both in and outside Louisiana. One day, on a visit to Liberty's Kitchen (a food-service-based social enterprise serving at-risk youths by providing life and job skills) for lunch, I spotted Brack in the kitchen, assisting/training in the cafe, and helping them develop a school lunch catering service. He also talked about a project for a restaurant on the river end of newly reinvigorated Oak Street. That project was/is Cowbell. On the upscale casual menu are a thick burger with fine toppings, fish tacos, hanger steak, adult grilled cheeses, and food that happens on a whim. The desserts are simple and satisfying. Cowbell is quirky, fun, and always busy. Brack and his wife Krista are also quirky and fun—and big community activists and supporters. Sometimes there is nothing so fine as going into Cowbell, ordering the organic chili and cheese fries and an ice-cold beer, then firing up Brack with the latest gossip. Best. Entertainment. Ever.

Louisiana Blue Crab Tamales with Charred Tomatillo Salsa & Fresh Avocados

PREPARED BY CHEF BRACK MAY

(MAKES 10–12 TAMALES)

20 or so corn husks, soaked overnight in warm water
Cabbage leaves, for lining steamer

For the charred salsa:

12 tomatillos
1 small Spanish onion
1 poblano pepper
2 jalapeño peppers
8 cloves garlic, halved
Chopped cilantro, to taste

Lime juice, to taste
Salt and pepper, to taste
1 orange, cut into segments
3 chipotle peppers, seeded, bloomed in hot water

For the crab filling:

1 ancho chile, bloomed in warm water
2 tablespoons cream
½ pound claw crabmeat, any type
½ pound jumbo lump crabmeat, more if you like

2 tablespoons butter

Juice of 1 lime

2 tablespoons chopped cilantro

Salt and pepper to taste

3 tablespoons gruyère

For the tamale dough:

1 cup seasoned stock (corn, chicken, or shrimp)

1½ cups dry masa

6 ounces butter, lard, or vegetable shortening, at room
    temperature

2 teaspoons baking powder

½ teaspoon salt

Kernels from 2 ears fresh shucked corn

2 tablespoons chopped cilantro

¼ cup grated cheese, preferably aged dry jack

For the avocado garnish:

3 large avocados, sliced

½ small red onion, chopped

¼ cup chopped cilantro

To make the charred salsa: Remove husks from tomatillos. Chop tomatillos and onion roughly, and place in a bowl. Remove seeds from poblano pepper and one of the jalapeños. In a broiler or on a grill, char the peppers until blistered but not totally incinerated. Leaving the charred skin on, puree the peppers and garlic then add to the bowl, along with cilantro, lime juice, salt, and pepper to taste. (This makes a great base for chunky salsa, too.) Fold in orange segments. Puree the chipotle peppers and stir them in. Cool and reserve.

To make the crab filling: Steep the ancho in the cream, and puree.

Sauté the crab gingerly in the butter. Add lime juice, cilantro, salt, and pepper. Loosen mixture with the ancho-cream puree, allow to cool, then fold in the cheese. Reseason and chill in the refrigerator until cold.

To make the tamale dough: Warm the stock and stir in the dry masa. (This equals 2 cups fresh masa). Leave to cool.

Whip the fat until white and fluffy. Add the baking powder, then the masa, and blend. Add the salt, corn, cilantro, and cheese and whip for three minutes.

To make the tamales: As you take each husk from the soaking water, clean it out as needed, wiping with a damp towel to rid it of the corn silk.

Place a tablespoon of masa mixture in the middle of the husk and flatten out with wet fingers. Place a good tablespoon of the crab filling in the middle of the masa and slowly roll and fold each side over till the filling is mostly covered with the masa mixture. Fold the husk over and completely cover the masa to protect it while steaming. If you need two husks, go ahead. Fold the bottom of the package back opposite from the seam.

Use cabbage leaves and a few husks to line the bottom of a steamer. With more cabbage leaves, make a mound in the center. Arrange the tamales folded side down, leaning at a 45-degree angle. Place the steamer in a tall pot, cover, and steam.

The tamales will get steamed for about 35 minutes and then need to rest for about 6 to 7 minutes before moving and/or eating. They can be cooked ahead and resteamed from cold without any ill effect.

To serve, rip the top of the husk off to expose the cooked tamale, drizzle with charred salsa, and top with avocado slices, red onion, and cilantro. Eat a couple before anyone sees that you have made them.

Sweet Potato Pecan Pie

(MAKES 6 INDIVIDUAL PIES)

For the pie dough:

¾ pound (3 sticks) cold unsalted butter
3 cups flour
⅓ cup sugar
½ teaspoon kosher salt
⅓ cup ice water, or less
1 egg, lightly beaten, for sealing rims
2–4 tablespoons heavy cream, for brushing

For the sweet potato filling:

4–5 sweet potatoes
2 tablespoons butter
5 ounces white sugar, plus 1 tablespoon for caramelizing

1 ounce all-purpose flour
¼ teaspoon ground cinnamon
⅛ teaspoon ground ginger
3 eggs
1 ounce maple syrup
1½ cups heavy cream

For the pecan "frangipane":

8 ounces pecans
8 ounces sugar
4 ounces butter
2 ounces all-purpose flour
2 egg yolks and 1 white
½ pound shelled whole pecans, for garnish

To make the dough: Cut the butter into ¼-inch dice and place in the freezer for 6 to 8 minutes. Remove and combine in a bowl with flour, sugar, and salt. Rub the butter and dry ingredients with your fingers to separate the butter pieces. Place in a food processor and pulse about 6 times. Slowly add enough ice water for the dough to ball up. Place on a floured surface and get the dough to come together without overworking. Wrap in plastic wrap and allow to rest for 1 hour in the refrigerator. Cut into 6 portions and ball up. Roll out on a floured surface into 5- to 6-inch disks about ¼ inch thick. Refrigerate again until ready to assemble.

To make the filling: Preheat oven to 325°F. Peel one small sweet potato and dice it. Wash the rest, pierce their skins, and place in the oven on a foil-lined tray. Put 1 tablespoon butter in a small baking dish in the oven. When it melts, toss diced sweet potato with the butter and 1 tablespoon sugar, and return to oven. Roast the dice until caramelized, and the whole sweet potatoes until soft. Remove and cool. Reserve dice for garnish.

Scoop potato flesh from skins and measure out 14 ounces. Place in bowl of mixer with remaining sugar and other ingredients. Blend, but do not whip, until smooth.

To make the "frangipane": Crush the pecans with the sugar in a food processor. Cream the butter into the nuts and sugar. Add the flour. When everything else is creamed, mix in the eggs with quick pulses.

Remove dough disks from fridge. Place a tablespoon of frangipane on the bottom of each disk and spread thin. Put a generous ¼ cup of sweet potato filling in the middle of the pie, leaving a 1-inch rim. Egg-wash the rim and then fold over, a small section at a time, until you have a little pie. Top with another tablespoon of the frangipane, some cooked sweet potato pieces, and a couple of pecans. Brush the pastry rim with heavy cream. Refrigerate the pies for 20 minutes.

Bake at 375° to 400°F for about 25 minutes, rotating once or twice. Cool for 10 minutes and eat warm, perhaps with some freshly whipped cream or vanilla ice cream.

DANTE'S KITCHEN

736 DANTE STREET
(504) 861-3121
DANTESKITCHEN.COM
EXECUTIVE CHEF: EMAN LOUBIER

Eman cut his teeth at Commander's Palace under the tutelage of the late chef Jamie Shannon. When he departed to open Dante's Kitchen, he described his restaurant as "upscale Louisiana fishing camp" and himself as a "sophisticated barbarian." Loathe to admit it, he's an aging hippie with a serious amount of smarts, integrity, and business acumen. He has never let food trends guide his craft or his menus and was the first chef

to have a blackboard highlighting all the local farmers and their produce for that evening's menu. There is always a vegetarian offering and an ethnic cuisine exploration. His Chicken Roasted under a Brick (maple glazed with a fried duck egg topping a potato-and-bacon hash cake) has been called "life changing." He is a staunch supporter of local farmers and fishermen. There is a Gulf fish dish or two on the menu, and the treatment is simple to set off the seafood's freshness. He loves to ferment, cure, can, and pickle meats, fruits, and vegetables— all are on display above the bar, on shelves over tables, and everywhere around the restaurant. Eman was one of the early adopters of the handcrafted cocktail movement, and his bartenders often incorporate the house's canned fruits and vegetables into stellar drinks. Eman is a voracious cookbook reader and ethnic food lover; both are reflected in the foods he eats (he loves to talk shop) and the dishes that appear on the menus. Dante's is legendary for its brunch, especially the extra creamy grits that sit under beef pan drippings and eggs, or come alongside mammoth grilled shrimp with an andouille redeye gravy. Several years ago he added pastry chef Kristyne Bouley to his staff, and everyone was smitten. Her desserts feel like home—fruit pies (sometimes straightforward, sometimes an unusual combination of savory done sweet), sorbets, cakes, crumbles, and more. Really, as much as the cuisine is a joy, there is always, always, always room for dessert.

REDFISH ON THE HALF SHELL WITH JUMBO LUMP CRABMEAT & SOFT HERBS

This dish is best if cooked on a grill outside or in a well-ventilated kitchen.

(SERVES 4)

4 redfish fillets, 8–10 ounces each, skin and scales
   left on

Olive oil to coat

1–2 tablespoons Creole seasoning mix

4 or 5 sprigs each of parsley, cilantro, tarragon, chervil,
   mint, and dill

½ pound jumbo lump crabmeat, picked over for shell

1 tablespoon extra virgin olive oil

1 teaspoon sugarcane vinegar, or any light-flavored
   vinegar

Juice of 1 lemon

Salt and pepper

Start a charcoal fire on the grill and let the coals settle down to a good hot red. Check your redfish for any remnants of rib bones. Lightly coat fish with oil and sprinkle with seasoning mix. Place the fillets on the grill, skin side down. Do not turn the fish over. We will cook it entirely on the skin side, thus preserving the moisture and not encumbering the fish with grill flavors. This will take 10 to 15 minutes on a hot grill.

While it is cooking, pick the herbs off the stems. Try to use the smaller leaves (you can use the larger leaves, just tear them up a little), then put the herbs into a bowl. Add the crabmeat. Toss with extra virgin olive oil, vinegar, lemon juice, and salt and pepper.

When the fish is done, place the fillets on plates and top with crab salad.

Pairs well with popcorn rice and a Chablis.

Green Tomato Pie Filling

(MAKES ONE 9-INCH PIE)

½ cup sugar

¼ cup all-purpose flour

1½ pounds medium green tomatoes, diced

5 ounces unsalted butter

2–3 tablespoons brandy

Zest of ½ lemon

Salt

Dash of vanilla

Splash of lemon juice

Combine sugar and flour in a bowl and toss with tomatoes. Melt 1 ounce butter in a skillet and saute tomatoes until they start to give up juice. (If they start to stick, turn down heat and add a little water.) Deglaze with brandy and cook until tender. Add remaining butter and lemon zest. Cool. Add salt, vanilla, and lemon juice to taste.

Fill a 9-inch pie shell, and bake like an apple pie. If the pie is going to be served hot, season the filling while it is hot. If it is going to be served cold or at room temperature, season the filling when cooler.

One Restaurant & Lounge

8132 Hampson Street
(504) 301-9061
ONERESTAURANTNOLA.COM
Executive Chef: Scott Snodgrass

Immediately through the front door, the kitchen is visible. Chef–co-owner Scott and his sous-chef are moving with balletic grace in the small, galleylike space. There are four or so seats at the kitchen's "bar table," and from there the perfectly ordered mise en place (prepared and cut garnishes and ingredients) can be seen. For those who care (me), it is breathtakingly precise, neat, and tidy. But before the diners are seated, co-owner Lee McCullough is the meeter and greeter, and the tall-tabled bar area beckons for a classic martini or kicked-up cocktail. Scott and Lee have crafted a lovely, lively restaurant. When they opened in 2004, it was to carve an original style and add to the élan of the Riverbend neighborhood. They met that goal and have held to it, consistently producing and evolving. Scott has called his menu "contemporary comfort food," and that's apt. Certain dishes stand firm: the Louisiana Char-Grilled Oysters with Roquefort and Red Wine Vinaigrette, or the Liver and Mushroom Pâté, for instance. Standout comfort dishes include Shrimp and Grits or a meaty Open-Face Brisket Sandwich with Shoestring Potatoes. At dinner, there is always a selection of beef, pork, fowl, and fish, elegantly prepared and garnished. Chef Scott also caters to a clientele with a lot of dietary requests that he happily accommodates. Luckily he has shared his outstanding gluten-free crab cakes and flourless chocolate cake.

Gluten-Free Crab Cakes

(SERVES 6–8)

3 egg yolks
1 whole egg
4 lemons, zested and juiced
1½–2 cups vegetable oil
½ cup honey
3 teaspoons salt
1 pound Louisiana lump crabmeat
1–2 tablespoons cooked mirepoix (see note)

Note: Mirepoix is a mixture of onion, carrot, and celery, usually in the ratio 2:1:1, cooked gently in butter or oil as a flavor base for soups and sauces.

Put egg yolks, whole egg, and lemon zest into a food processor and whip until egg mixture doubles in volume. With the motor still on, slowly drizzle the oil into the cup so that the oil and eggs emulsify. When about half of the oil is blended in, add the honey and about half of the lemon juice, then the rest of the oil and the salt. Taste the resulting aioli for a balance of sweetness, tartness, and saltiness. Add more honey or lemon, as you like, and put in refrigerator for 3 to 4 hours to chill.

Put crabmeat into a mixing bowl and combine with 2 tablespoons of the aioli and 2 tablespoons of mirepoix. Use an ice cream scoop or your hands to make six tight balls or cakes.

The cakes can be cooked in a nonstick skillet over low heat. Or you can spray a sheet pan with baking spray and bake the crab cakes in a 400°F oven for 10 to 12 minutes.

FLOURLESS MOLTEN CHOCOLATE CAKE

(SERVES 6–8)

½ pound unsalted butter, plus more to butter the cups

½ cup white sugar, plus more to coat the cups

6 whole eggs

6 egg yolks

2 cups semisweet chocolate

½ cup cognac or other brandy (optional)

Melt ½ pound butter in a bowl set over boiling water. Butter the insides of 6 coffee cups or large ramekins and dust with sugar. Put eggs and ½ cup sugar into the bowl of a stand mixer and whip until doubled in volume. Meanwhile, add chocolate and brandy to butter mixture, stirring carefully until all is melted together, then add to the egg mix.

Pour batter into sugared cups about two-thirds to three-quarters full. Bake in a 400°F convection oven for 7 to 8 minutes. For conventional ovens, increase temperature to 450°F and cook for 10 to 12 minutes. Let cool for 4 hours at room temperature, then "pop" the cakes out of the cups.

Reheat in oven for 2 to 3 minutes, or microwave for 20 to 30 seconds, and serve with whipped cream and berries.

Truburger

8115 Oak Street

(504) 218-5416

truburgernola.com

Chef: Aaron Burgau; Chef/General Manager: Via Fortier

Among the first of the burger joint creators on the New Orleans food scene, Chef Aaron had a vision for fresh, handmade burgers, done simply and well, some creative topping options, a great hot dog, locally made hamburger buns, thick milk shakes, and thin, crispy fries to drag through his house-created Worchestershire-spiked "tru sauce." Mission accomplished. The restaurant's chef–general manager, Via Fortier, is a force with a voice. She runs a tight ship. She uses that voice to call out orders, and there is no missing her Mississippi twang. Truburger seeks to be nothing more than it is as burger joints go: family friendly, food discounts for students, a variety of special burgers like The Truth (beef patty, thin fried onion rings, Swiss cheese, and "tru sauce"), battered onion rings, and when the mood strikes, chicken wings that Aaron smokes at his fine-dine restaurant (Patois) to be served with a homemade spicy ranch dressing. Serious about casual food done with care, they hired Taylor Noble, a "burger butcher" who hand-cuts, grinds, and forms beef patties daily. Chefs Aaron and Via together created the impossibly fantastic veggie burger packed with beets, beans, and brown rice; a dense and delicious gluten-free burger bun; and the recipe they share here for their fluffy, hand-dipped corn dog batter.

Corn Dog Batter

"At Truburger, we dip all-beef Zweigle's hot dogs into this batter and fry them golden," says Via. "If you can't get Zweigle's hot dogs, use your favorite brand."

(MAKES 8–10)

2 cups flour

2 cups cornmeal

½ cup sugar

3 teaspoons baking powder

2 teaspoons baking soda

1½ teaspoons salt

2½ cups buttermilk

2 eggs

Mix all dry ingredients together. Add buttermilk and eggs to dry mixture, and whisk to combine. If you do not use it immediately, you may need to add more buttermilk later.

Ye Olde College Inn

3000 South Carrollton Avenue
(504) 866-3683
collegeinn1933.com
Executive Chef: Brad McGehee

Ye Olde College Inn is not only a restaurant, it's a happening, an event, a landmark. People of an age remember the days of carhop service, "parking," po-boys and familiar plates of hamburger steak, breaded veal cutlets, chicken-fried steak, red beans and rice, and pickled beet salad. The restaurant was opened in 1933 by the Rufin family and held by them until 2003, when the Blancher family bought College Inn. Two years into the Blanchers' restaurant ownership, and after restoring the damage done by

Hurricane Katrina, they moved their popular bowling lanes and music venue, Rock 'n' Bowl, from Tulane Avenue to Carrollton, immediately abutting the "new" College Inn. A handful of the old items are still on the menu, right alongside a wider range of new dishes created by Johnny Blancher Jr. and Executive Chef Brad McGehee. Today, much of the food includes ingredients plucked from the restaurant's nearby raised-bed gardens or local farmers markets. The Blanchers love to say, "College Inn and Rock 'n' Bowl is your one-stop place to dine and rock." As we say in New Orleans, "True dat."

SWEET POTATO–ANDOUILLE SOUP

(SERVES 10–12)

½ pound andouille sausage, diced

2 onions, diced

3 ounces Grand Marnier

3 sweet potatoes, peeled and diced

1 ounce honey

½ teaspoon cayenne pepper

1 teaspoon cinnamon

1 bay leaf

½ gallon whole milk

Salt and pepper to taste

Brown the diced sausage in a 3-gallon stockpot. Add diced onions and sweat until translucent. Add Grand Marnier and reduce until almost dry. Add sweet potatoes and 2 quarts water. Bring to a simmer and cook for 35 minutes or until potatoes are soft. Add honey, cayenne, cinnamon, and bay leaf. With an immersion blender, or working in batches with a food processor, blend soup mixture until smooth. Add milk, and season with salt and pepper. Serve hot.

EAT MORE BACON
PULLED PORK SHOULDER
LOIN IS FOR LOVERS
BABY GOT BACK RIBS
PIG-LICIOUS
BACON yummm!
HAPPY HAM = HAPPY (WO)MAN!

MID-CITY

Crescent Pie & Sausage

4400 Banks Street
(504) 482-2426
CRESCENTPIEANDSAUSAGE.COM
Executive Chef/Owner: Bart Bell; Co-Owner: Jeff Baron

On Banks Street, several blocks off Carrollton and directly behind Jesuit High School, is the very neighborhoody neighborhood location of this restaurant. Chef-owners Bart Bell and Jeff Baron built the place from the ground up, using reclaimed wood as well as both found and new objects. Bart has a strong fine-dine history, but being a native Louisianan and with serious adoration and respect for the regional cuisine, he partnered with business- and pizza-savvy Jeff to open their doors. Best known for the jambalaya stuffed with copious amounts of house-smoked meats and studded with toothy black-eyed peas, Crescent Pie is also revered for the sausages and boudin, all made on site. Nontraditional, beautifully chewy and crusty pizzas are Jeff's contribution to the menu, and the place is pure fun, including Saturdays for serious brunch (also thank you to Jeff). Cold craft beers on tap and in bottles, fun cocktails, and great food—Jeff and Bart ask, "What more could you want?" Not. A. Single. Thing.

DUCK CONFIT MEAT PIES

(MAKES 8–10 HAND PIES)

For the dough:

½ pound unsalted butter
2½ cups all purpose four
2 tablespoons sugar
1 teaspoon salt
½ cup iced water
½ teaspoon white wine vinegar

For the filling:

¼ cup bacon grease
2 leeks, white part only, chopped
2 cups sliced cremini mushrooms
¼ teaspoon salt
¼ teaspoon pepper
1 cup ricotta
1 egg, lightly beaten
½ pound confit duck thigh meat (any recipe), pulled
 from bone
Vegetable oil for frying

To make the dough: Cut the butter into cubes and freeze for about 10 minutes.

In the large bowl of a mixer with a paddle attachment, sift together the flour, sugar, and salt. Once it is well blended, add the butter and mix on low speed for 2 minutes. Stop the machine and pinch any large pieces until flattened.

Combine the iced water and vinegar and then add the mixture to the dough all at once while on low speed. The consistency after this should be tacky but not too moist.

Take dough out of bowl, wrap in plastic film, and refrigerate for at least 2 hours or, much better, until the next day.

Remove from the fridge and roll out into ¼-inch flat sheet. Using a 5-inch-diameter cookie cutter, cut out circles and discard the extra dough. Now you have your dough disks to make the pies! (Return to fridge if not using immediately.)

To make the filling: Put bacon grease in a large black cast iron skillet. Saute leeks over medium-low heat until golden brown, then add mushrooms and cook until mushrooms are cooked but not mushy. Salt and pepper to taste. Remove from pan and cool.

Add ricotta to cooled leeks and mushrooms and mix with your hands until the mixture is consistent.

To assemble meat pies: Take the dough disks out of the fridge and place on the table. (It's much easier to handle the dough when it's cool to room temperature. Once the dough gets any warmer, it can get gooey and very difficult to work with).

Wipe the rim of each disk with egg wash. Spoon about 1 tablespoon of the leek-mushroom-ricotta mixture onto the center of the disk. Then add a nice big pinch of duck—there should be just a little bit more mixture than duck meat. Fold the dough over to enclose the duck and mixture inside. Crimp the edges down.

Once all the pies are assembled, arrange on a cookie sheet with parchment paper underneath (be careful that the pies are not touching one another) and place in the freezer. When the pies have solidified, after approximately 2 hours, take out and place in fridge.

Heat a pot of vegetable oil to 355°F. Submerge pies in the pot of oil and be careful not to crowd the pot. Let cook for roughly 7 minutes or until golden brown. Take out and let cool for 30 seconds . . . and then EAT!!!

Ralph's on the Park

900 City Park Avenue
(504) 488-1000
RALPHSONTHEPARK.COM
Executive Chef: Chip Flanagan
Executive Pastry Chef: Brett Gauthier

Ralph Brennan's namesake restaurant is gorgeous. Sharply appointed, painted in soothing colors, and encased by large plate glass windows that look upon the giant moss-hung oak trees and greenery of City Park. He's been in the business since he was a teenager, and as a part of an eponymous restaurant family, Ralph's on the Park is one of his eight "babies." Ralph describes this restaurant as "globally inspired local cuisine." At the kitchen helm is the equally passionate executive chef Chip Flanagan. Chip's food is serious, yet playful—Roof Bacon (rooftop-smoked bacon with fresh local pea shoots) is among his many creative creations. A passionate advocate for local and regional products, Chip is often spotted at local farmers markets, shopping, eating, and on occasion dishing up a Green Plate Special. He has a great sense of humor, is laid back, fun, and smart. One of his shining attributes is being comfortable with both local and ethnic cuisines, and his menu reflects sensible updates to New Orleans favorites with eclectic twists. "Brunch on the Park" is a perfect example of tweaked tradition—Turtle Soup followed by Braised Lamb (lamb ragout, cream cheese grits, fried egg, redeye gravy) and a finale of White Chocolate Bread Pudding. The recipes he's offered here further show off his playful style: ramped-up bivalves with Latin flair paired with pork, and a New Orleans favorite treat, a sno-ball, gone sophisticated.

Masa Fried Oysters with
Crispy Pork Belly & Lemon Sauce

(SERVES 4 AS APPETIZER)

For the pork belly:

½ cup salt
½ cup sugar
1 slab pork belly, skinless (can use thick-cut bacon)

For the lemon sauce:

3 large lemons
1 cup cane sugar
6 ounces cane vinegar
Pinch of salt and pepper

For the masa fried oysters:

Cooking oil, as needed
1 cup masa flour
2 teaspoons salt
1 teaspoon ground black pepper
12 oysters
12 (1-ounce) slices slow-roasted pork belly
4 ounces lemon sauce
Sweet corn sprouts, for garnish

To make the pork belly: Combine salt and sugar and sprinkle all over the pork belly. Place curing belly in a plastic bag and refrigerate. Let belly cure overnight. The next day, preheat the oven to 250°F. Remove belly from bag and wipe off any cure that remains. Place belly in a roasting pan and cover with a lid or foil. Slow-roast the pork belly until the internal temperature reaches 165°F. This will take several hours; do not rush it. When temperature is reached, remove the belly from the oven and let cool in the roasting pan. When it is cool enough to handle, place in the refrigerator for a few hours. When it is fully chilled, it can be easily sliced. Slice off a strip of belly and cut 1 ounce portions. Repeat until there are 12 rectangles.

Refrigerate the rest of the slab and use it with everything. For a treat, roast the belly on top of peeled carrots . . . delicious.

To make the lemon sauce: Remove the rind and white pith from the lemons. Place pulp and juice in a saucepot with the sugar, vinegar, and 1 cup water. Bring to a boil. Turn heat down to a simmer and cook for 30 minutes, or until a syrupy consistency is achieved. Strain out pulp and seeds and discard. Season the sauce with salt and pepper.

To make the fried oysters: In a heavy skillet, pour cooking oil to a depth of ½ inch. Set over medium-high heat. If using a thermometer, heat oil to 360° to 370°F.

Season the masa with the salt and pepper. Dredge the oysters in the seasoned masa. Drop a small pinch of masa in the oil. If it sizzles and bubbles, then the oil is ready. Carefully place the oysters in the oil, one at a time. Cook for about 90 seconds, turn the oysters over, and cook for 1 minute more. Remove the oysters from the oil and drain on layers of paper towels.

Place the slices of pork belly in the same oil and cook until browned and crisp, about 3 minutes. Remove the belly and drain with the oysters.

To serve, spoon lemon sauce onto four plates. Set 3 pork belly slices on each plate and set oysters on the belly pieces. Garnish with sweet corn sprouts.

STUFFED PEACH SNO-BALL

(SERVES 8)

For the peach granita:

2 cups ripe peaches, pitted

2 cups iced water

⅓ cup sugar

2 tablespoons lemon juice

Pinch of salt

For the sparkling sabayon cream:

7 egg yolks

⅓ cup sugar

1½ tablespoons honey

2 cups sparkling wine

½ cup cream

For the assembly:

8 ripe peaches

8 martini glasses

8 mint leaves, for garnish

To make the granita: Combine all ingredients in a blender until smooth. Pass through a fine mesh strainer. Adjust seasoning with lemon, salt, or sugar. Pour into a shallow pan and place in the freezer. Stir mixture with a fork every 30 minutes until frozen.

The granita can be made a day in advance. When ready to serve, remove from freezer and let sit for 10 minutes. Scrape with a fork into ice crystals.

To make the cream: First prepare an ice bath, and set a pot of water to boil. Choose a bowl or basin that will sit on the pot of water. In it combine the yolks, sugar, and honey and whisk until lighter in color. Add wine to yolk mixture. Place bowl over pot of boiling water. Whisk over heat until mixture becomes thick and airy. Chill mixture over ice bath, occasionally stirring gently.

In a chilled bowl, whip the cream to medium-peak consistency, and fold it into the chilled Sabayon.

This component should be prepared as close to serving time as possible, as it will begin to lose volume.

To assemble: Peel and dice the 8 peaches and distribute in the bottom of the martini glasses. Top the diced peaches with sabayon cream, but be sure to leave room for peach granita. Fill the glass with granita as high as possible, to resemble a New Orleans Sno-Ball. Garnish with a mint leaf and serve immediately.

Toups' Meatery

845 North Carrollton Avenue
(504) 252-4999
TOUPSMEATERY.COM
Executive Chef: Isaac Toups

With more than ten years in fine dining, Chef Isaac Toups craved to break out on his own and cook up sophisticated (but not too sophisticated) Louisiana dishes. Finally scoring a building that was once a Mediterranean restaurant on a busy stretch of Carrollton Avenue near City Park, Isaac and his wife Amanda renovated and opened this clean, blond-wood-bedecked restaurant bursting with creative and recognizable dishes from Isaac's hometown of Rayne, Louisiana. After only a few months, Toups' Meatery received high marks from local food writers for the house-cured charcuterie, crispy-fatty-fabulous cracklin's, pickles, massive cuts of meat, po-boys, and plates of stewy, slow-cooked foods. Isaac runs a tight, silent kitchen; his intensity is demonstrated in the plates of food that pour forth. Amanda is the "show girl," bubbling with personality at the front of house. The restaurant is consistently busy, with good reason. Amanda says, "We knew Isaac was good, that his food was good, though we didn't have a clue we'd be this popular this quickly. It's exciting!" Yes, it is.

Confit Chicken Thighs, Butter Beans, Greens & Gizzard Gravy

(SERVES 4)

For the chicken:

4 chicken quarters, ribs removed
Kosher salt and black pepper
2 tablespoons fresh rosemary, finely chopped
2 tablespoons thyme
2 tablespoons oregano
10 cloves garlic
Duck fat as needed
Peanut oil as needed

For the beans:

1 tablespoon canola oil
1 onion, diced
2 ribs celery, diced
1 bell pepper, diced

6 strips smoked bacon, cut into 1-inch strips
2 bay leaves
1 pound dried butter beans
2–4 quarts chicken stock, as needed
Salt and cayenne pepper
2 tablespoons unsalted butter

For the greens:

1 tablespoon canola oil
2 cloves garlic, minced
Pinch of crushed red pepper flakes
1 bunch mustard greens
Pinch of salt
Juice of 1 lemon

For the gravy:

¼ cup flour

¼ cup canola oil

1 small onion, diced

2 cups chicken stock

6 ounces dark beer

1 pound chicken gizzards, cleaned and minced

1 teaspoon toasted ground cumin

1 tablespoon smoked paprika

Salt and pepper to taste

To make the confit of chicken: **Season chicken generously with kosher salt and black pepper. Finely chop all herbs and garlic and mix well. Rub garlic and herb mixture into each side of thighs. Cover and refrigerate for 24 hours.**

Place chicken in a baking dish or Dutch oven large enough to fit all thighs with 2 inches of clearance at the top. Completely cover chicken with equal parts rendered duck fat and peanut oil. Place in 225°F oven for two hours or until chicken is falling off the bone.

Remove with slotted spatula and place on plates. If not serving immediately, allow to cool, and reheat in fat.

To cook the beans: **In a large Dutch oven, heat canola oil on medium heat. Sweat onion, celery, and bell pepper for 2 minutes, add bacon and cook for 1 minute more. Add bay leaves, beans, and enough chicken stock to cover by 3 inches. Bring mixture to a boil, taste water, and add salt and cayenne to taste. Lower to a simmer and let cook 2½ to 3 hours. Stir in butter right before serving.**

To cook the greens: **Heat canola oil on medium heat. Sauté garlic until golden brown, approximately 1 minute. Add pepper flakes, greens, and salt. Wilt for 1 minute until cooked through. Add lemon juice and serve.**

To make the gravy: **Cook flour and oil to make a light roux the color of café au lait. Sweat onions in the roux for 1 minute. Add chicken stock and beer, and bring to a boil. Add gizzards (Isaac grinds his gizzards in a meat grinder, but that may not be an option for most home cooks), cumin, paprika, and salt and pepper to taste. Lower fire to a simmer and cook for 2 hours.**

MARIGNY
&
BYWATER

Bacchanal

600 Poland Avenue
(504) 948-9111
Bacchanalwine.com
Executive Chef: Joaquin Rodas

The weatherworn building that is Bacchanal began as a cool wineshop located at the far end of the Bywater district. The space has a wine cave feel, and the juice is handpicked by wine guru Chris Rudge. Back in the day, Bacchanal offered wine classes, as well as fine hard liquors, eventually adding cheeses and pâtés to the menu. There were lazy Sunday evenings when Bacchanal held chill parties with live local music. Hungry patrons were known to saunter over to the Joint for fantastic, smoky barbecue to go, and all was right with the world. In late summer–early fall 2005, as Bacchanal reopened, infamous local chef Pete Vazquez (onetime chef-owner of late lamented Marisol) began cooking up a series of cool ethnic eats on those Sunday evenings—among the first of the local underground or "speakeasy" dining experiences—and his delicious antics, many locals know, were the impetus for a character in the HBO series *Treme.* Bacchanal subsequently curried a random and rotating gaggle of chefs on the grill for these rogue cookouts. Then came some city permit wrangling and the establishment

of regular dining service with the cookery of Chef Joaquin Rodas. Joaquin's food was familiar to in-the-know New Orleanians who'd tasted his dishes during his time at Mimi's in the Marigny. Eclectic bistro fare best describes the food at Bacchanal, where there is ceviche, bacon-wrapped dates, seasonal soups, and a host of hearty entrees like whole branzino, flatiron steak, confit chicken thighs, and, for this book, Joaquin's deep, dusky stew-soup pozole. Want something sweet to get that dance mojo working? The chocolate bark is salty-sweet goodness.

BRAISED PORK SHOULDER POZOLE

(SERVES 4–6)

2 pounds pork shoulder, cut into fist-size cubes

Salt and pepper

4 tablespoons canola oil

10 cloves garlic, peeled

3 yellow onions, sliced

1 pint grape tomatoes

2 bottles Mexican beer

2 cups chicken stock

1 medium (28-ounce) can white hominy, drained and rinsed

2 sprigs cilantro

2 tablespoons Mexican oregano, plus more for garnish

½ head iceberg lettuce, thinly sliced

2 white onions, sliced, marinated in white vinegar for 1 hour

1 bunch cilantro, chopped

4 limes, quartered

Pat the pork pieces dry with paper towels. Sprinkle generously with salt and pepper. In a large overproof braising pan, heat canola oil, enough to coat the bottom, on medium-high heat. Working in batches, taking care not to crowd the pan or stir much, brown the meat on all sides. Once it has browned, transfer it to a bowl.

Preheat oven to 300°F.

Add garlic, onions, and grape tomatoes to pan. Stir well so as to not let anything burn. Once the onions and tomatoes start to release water, stir less frequently. Cook until onions are translucent, then add the beer. Reduce beer by half, add the chicken stock, and bring to a boil. Return the pork to the pan. Bring back to a boil, cover with a tight-fitting lid or aluminum foil, and place in the oven for 4 hours.

After 2 hours add the rinsed hominy, cilantro sprigs, 2 tablespoons oregano, and 1 tablespoon salt. Return to oven for remaining 2 hours, after which the pork should be fork tender and have a nice caramelized hue.

Divide the pozole on serving plates. Garnish with shaved iceberg lettuce, marinated onions, cilantro, and lime wedges. Finish with a shower of Mexican oregano rubbed between your hands.

DARK CHOCOLATE BARK

(MAKES 1 1/4 POUNDS OF BARK)

2 cups bittersweet chocolate (54% cocoa is ideal),
 chopped into small pieces
¾ cup roasted and peeled Marcona almonds
5 tablespoons extra virgin olive oil
2 tablespoons top-quality sea salt, such as Maldon or
 fleur de sel
Pinch of chile threads or cayenne pepper (optional)

Place a pot of water on the stove on medium-high heat. Once water starts to boil, place a metal mixing bowl on top of the pot. Choose a bowl that fits deeply in the pot, yet covers the rim so as to keep the steam from escaping. Put chopped chocolate in the bowl and melt it.

In a food processor, pulse the almonds until they are finely chopped, almost dust. Once chocolate is melted, fold in the almonds and incorporate completely.

Place parchment paper on a baking sheet, using adhesive tape to keep the paper at bay. Carefully remove the bowl of melted chocolate from the pot of boiling water and pour about half the chocolate onto the baking sheet. With a spatula, spread the chocolate until it is very thin. (Put some back into the bowl if necessary.) Set the baking sheet in the refrigerator, level, until chocolate hardens completely. Repeat with remaining chocolate.

To plate, break chocolate into jagged shards, place on plates, drizzle with extra virgin olive oil, and strew with salt and, if you like, chile threads.

Cake Café & Bakery

2440 Chartres Street
(504) 943-0010
NOLACAKES.COM
Executive Chef: Steve Himelfarb

This corner bakery cum cafe evokes the feeling of being in a beloved aunt's kitchen, where warm yeast scents are heavy on the air, coffee is brewing, and cupcakes tempt from the pastry case. Chef Steve started his culinary tenure as "the cake man" selling fat individual cake slices to patrons and businesses along Magazine Street. Roll forward a number of years, and a short time at a teeny space on Exchange Alley in the French Quarter, to his current Marigny digs. Here, along with the pastries, there are giant, fluffy biscuits piled with eggs and ham, omelets, grits, tofu scramble, fried oyster sandwiches (when oysters are in season), meatloaf, salads, and all manners of soul-satisfying soups. One of Steve's famous cupcakes can be added to any meat for a dollar; the difficulty is in choosing from among the daily flavors that can include double chocolate, wedding cake, mimosa, red velvet, or even Sazerac. Always innovating, Chef Steve and his bakery team came up with Mardi Gras's wildly popular, bold purple-green-and-gold-icing-striped King Cakes filled with goat cheese and apples. Year round, spot hilariously decadent items in the case like the walnut-filled Buddha Hands, the Deep-Fried Chocolate Croissant, or the genius Quichant that can be a carnivore's or herbivore's dream. Steve shared the Quichant because "They are seriously delicious and probably the most fun thing someone would want to make at home."

QUICHANT

Making homemade croissant and puff pastry is a labor of love, and a labor. If you're committed to the process, that's incredible, but for this recipe Chef Steve says that store-bought dough and puff pastry tart shells are perfectly wonderful.

(SERVES 10–12)

10–12 best-quality frozen puff pastry tart shells
10–12 best-quality store-bought croissant or fine
   crescent-roll dough
12 eggs
½ cup half-and-half

Optional filling ingredients:

Bacon, cooked and crumbled
Cheddar cheese, grated
Red or yellow onion, diced
Roasted red peppers
Fresh goat cheese, crumbled

Fold croissant/crescent roll dough to fit into the bottom of the tart shell. Place on parchment lined cookie sheet. Chill for 30 minutes.

While the dough-lined tart shells are chilling, gather your filling ingredients—perhaps bacon, cheddar, and onion for the carnivores or roasted red peppers, goat cheese, and onion for vegetarians—about 2 tablespoons altogether per tart. Put fillings into shells and chill again for 15 minutes.

Whip the eggs together with the half-and-half. Pour mixture into the shells, over fillings, almost to the top of the shell. Bake quichants at 350°F for 20 to 25 minutes, until top is golden and filling is firm but slightly wobbly. Cool and serve warm or at room temperature.

Elizabeth's

601 Gallier Street
(504) 944-9272
ELIZABETHSRESTAURANTNOLA.COM
Executive Chef: Bryon Peck

If there is one thing people know about Elizabeth's, it's the praline bacon. To be sure, it's very, very good, but Chef Bryon Peck is about more than praline bacon, even if that was what put Elizabeth's on the map. Adhering to the original owner's philosophy of "Real food, done real good," Bryon has long cooked or cooked-and-managed at Elizabeth's,

and it finally and officially became his in 2011. The hundred-year-old building functioned as a catering kitchen in 1996, then a restaurant, went through a succession of owners, and now, fully in Bryon's hands, has really hit its culinary stride. The menu is broad-ranging at breakfast, lunch, dinner, and brunch, with everything from burgers to seafood, French toast, and cocktails. The fried chicken livers with homemade pepper jelly are astounding, and there is crazy love for the strawberry-stuffed French toast, the Dream Burger with praline bacon and blue cheese (ooh, that sweet-tangy-salty thing), and fork-tender pork osso bucco over a fried grit cake. The huge menu also boasts crab cakes, frog legs, scallops, fish, meat, and at brunch a Duck Waffle (sweet potato and duck hash atop a cornbread waffle) or these hunger-inducing dishes for which Bryon has generously provided his recipes.

Baked Oysters with Foie Gras & Truffle Aioli

Combining briny local bivalves and the richness of foie gras (happily not banned in New Orleans) with a wee drizzle of truffle oil, this is nothing but utter decadence.

(SERVES 6–8)

10 ounces foie gras

4 egg yolks

1 tablespoon Dijon mustard

Juice of 1 lemon

2 ounces good-quality truffle oil

Salt

24 P&J oysters in the shell

Start by rendering the foie over slow heat in a thick-bottomed pot, not allowing it to color. This will take at least 30 minutes. Remove foie from heat when fully rendered. Let set and cool until it reaches 120°F.

Start making aioli, in a Cuisinart or in a bowl with a stick blender, by blending the yolks with the mustard and lemon juice. Now slowly add truffle oil, then foie gras fat. As it thickens, thin with water. At the end add all rendered foie gras and its fat; again remember to thin out with water—perhaps 2 ounces in all. Finish by adding salt to taste.

Open oysters and loosen them from their shells, keeping each in its bottom shell-half. Top with aioli and put under broiler until sauce is golden and oysters are warm.

SALMON & BRIE GRILLED CHEESE
TOPPED WITH FRIED EGGS

(SERVES 4)

For the grilled cheese:

8 slices seeded rye bread
8 ounces brie cheese
6 ounces smoked Nova salmon, approximately 4 slices
Butter as needed

For the eggs:

Butter for frying
8 fresh eggs
Curly parsley, chopped, for garnish
Red onion, minced, for garnish

To make the sandwiches: Remove crusts from the bread and cut each slice into two rectangles. Lay bread on a cutting board. Cut brie into sixteen equal pieces and place on bread rectangles. Cut salmon into eight equal pieces and place them on half of the brie-topped bread slices. Fold over the other eight halves of brie-topped bread onto them to make sandwiches. Butter both sides of sandwiches generously, and grill.

To cook the eggs: In a nonstick skillet, melt butter. Fry eggs over easy. Place on top of grilled cheese sandwiches and garnish with chopped parsley and onion.

Maurepas Foods

3200 Burgundy Street
(504) 267-0072
MAUREPASFOODS.COM
Executive Chef: Mike Doyle
Executive Pastry Chef: Jessica Stokes

Chef Mike Doyle started his New Orleans career at Dante's Kitchen, where, much to his chagrin, he was sometimes called "the pickle whisperer." His grandmother's heavily clove-scented recipe for pickled beans made a perfect garnish for a Bloody Mary. But Mike had long wanted to operate his own restaurant, and so when the opportunity arose, Mike dived in, buying a historic Bywater building that needed a lot of TLC but was suitably situated in a part of town ripe for reinvigoration. In early 2012 the doors to Maurepas Foods flew open. Painted in warm colors, with many architectural details left intact, and adding a snazzy bar with truly innovative from-the-kitchen ingredients, the restaurant was an immediate hit not only with its own neighborhood residents but with plenty of food fanatics from across New Orleans. Using the tagline "purveyors of robust cuisine," Chef Mike and his staff put out share plates of slow-cooked greens studded with smoky meats, other vegetables lesser known to New Orleans palates, thoughtful preparations of seasonal, locally sourced produce, meats, seafood, and fowl, and creamy grits so delectable, they're criminal. Add to that the inventive contemporary-classic desserts of Jessica Stokes (an Emeril's veteran), bartender-mixologist Brad Smith's killer concoctions, and late night hours for a superior and successful restaurant recipe. And, Chef Mike is still making pickles—including those beans. There is a Bloody Mary calling out to be garnished . . .

Maurepas Foods Kohlrabi
(SERVES 12)

2 tablespoons vegetable oil

1 pound andouille sausage, chopped into half-rounds ¼ inch thick

8 cups kohlrabi, in ¾-inch dice

2 cups diced yellow onion

1½ cups brown sugar

½ cup Creole mustard

1 quart vegetable stock (homemade or store-bought)

Chopped parsley, for garnish

In a large saucepan, heat vegetable oil and cook the andouille. When brown spots form, add the diced kohlrabi and onions and sauté to a golden hue. Add the brown sugar and cook until it becomes bubbly and syrupy, then add the Creole mustard; stir well. Pour in the vegetable stock and simmer for about 25 minutes, stirring often, until the liquid is reduced to about 1 cup.

Serve as a side on its own, or over rice. Garnish with fresh parsley.

Maurepas Snack Cake

(YIELDS 28; MAY BE HALVED)

For the cakes:

3 cups coffee
1½ cups unsweetened cocoa powder
8 ounces 73% bittersweet chocolate
4 whole eggs
2 yolks
4½ cups sugar
5 teaspoons baking soda
¾ cup buttermilk
2 cups sour cream
2¼ cups vegetable oil
1½ tablespoons vanilla extract
5 cups all-purpose flour, sifted
1 tablespoon kosher salt

For the crème fraîche filling:

1 cup buttermilk
1 cup cream

For the chocolate frosting:

1½ pounds unsalted butter, melted
2 pounds bittersweet chocolate
10 cups powdered sugar, sifted
1 cup coffee, cooled
2 cups sour cream
1 tablespoon kosher salt
1 tablespoon vanilla

To make the cakes: Whisk together the coffee and cocoa powder in a small pot over low heat until hot and slightly thickened. In a bowl, place the chocolate, chopped fine. Pour mixture over chocolate. Stir to combine, then set aside to cool.

Preheat oven to 325°F. Line four 9-inch cake pans with buttered and floured parchment paper; set aside.

In the bowl of a stand mixer fitted with a whisk attachment, whisk the eggs and yolks. Combine sugar and baking soda, then gradually add to eggs, whisking until mixture is pale and thick. Add buttermilk, sour cream, vegetable oil, and vanilla, whisking well and scraping the bowl as you go. Transfer this mixture to a large mixing bowl and whisk in the sifted flour and salt.

Add the cooled chocolate mixture; whisk well and then pour into prepared cake pans. Bake for 20 to 30 minutes, rotating halfway through. Cakes are done when a toothpick comes out clean.

Turn out the cakes and cool completely. Wrap in plastic and chill 5 minutes in the freezer. With a 3-inch cookie cutter or ring mold, cut out cake rounds. With a smaller cutter, cut partway down and hollow out a well in the cakes' center to hold the crème fraîche filling

To make the filling: Whisk buttermilk and cream together well. Cover and set at room temperature for 36 to 48 hours, or until thickened. Whisk again, transfer into a clean container, and refrigerate.

To make the frosting: Pour warm melted butter over the chocolate and whisk to combine. One cup at a time, whisk in the powdered sugar—it will look "broken." Keep whisking and add in the coffee, then the sour cream. The mixture will come together at this point. Whisk in the salt and vanilla.

To assemble: Fill snack cakes with a bit of the crème fraîche, then frost as desired to cover each cake's top or pipe large dots.

Satsuma Cafe

3218 Dauphine Street, (504) 304-5962
7901 Maple Street, (504) 309-5557
satsumacafe.com
Executive Chef: Michael Costantini

In 2009 when Cassi and Peter Dymond opened Satsuma Cafe in the former Coffea space, they kept the vibe pretty much as it was, with simple breakfast items, sandwiches, and so on. They did evolve the menu some, adding fresh juices and farmers market produce, eventually hiring white-tablecloth-pedigreed chef Michael Costantini to take the food up a notch. These days, to call Satsuma Cafe a coffee shop

is to give it short shrift. Though the menu is composed of breakfasts, salads, sandwiches, and fresh-pressed juices of locally sourced produce, there is a gourmet quality to the offerings that elevates the cafe's status—evidence the inclusion of chanterelles in egg dishes or lump crabmeat that dolls up a grilled cheese. The funky-eclectic interior remains the same, with mismatched tables, wild art, and all manner of reading materials strewn about, giving Satsuma its hippie chic feel. For a time, the gang added dinner service that drew solid notices, but sadly it didn't stick, and so they dropped the evening menu of stylish dishes, had Michael refine the menu, and began searching for a second location to do more and bigger at breakfast and lunch. In August 2012, Satsuma's Uptown location opened with Chef Michael's gentle menu refinements. The possibility of doing dinner looms, but for now there are simple, lovely dishes that even have fans like food-obsessed Michael Stipe of R.E.M. who wrote this: "Their Kale Salad . . . Lacinato kale, Parmesan dressing and (this is New Orleans after all) a piece of bacon on the side . . . is the BEST SALAD in the city, hands down." Chef Michael gave up another of his salad recipes and a herbaceous, fruity cobbler too.

Warm Winter Salad of Roasted, Pickled & Raw Vegetables

(SERVES 6–8)

For the lemon vinaigrette:

¼ cup lemon juice
Zest of 2 lemons
1 teaspoon Dijon mustard
1 clove of garlic, microplaned
1 teaspoon chopped thyme
Pinch of salt
¼ cup canola oil
¼ cup extra virgin olive oil

For the pickled beet and red onion:

1 cup red wine vinegar
1 cup sugar
1 red beet, sliced
1 red onion, sliced thin

For the capers:

2 tablespoons capers, rinsed and dried
¼–½ cup canola oil

For the salad:

10 brussels sprouts
1 bunch Tuscan kale
¼ cup pickled red onion
½ butternut squash, top half only, peeled
2 carrots, peeled
2 parsnips, peeled
1 teaspoon salt
1 teaspoon pepper
1 tablespoon olive oil
4 (1½-inch) florets cauliflower
4 (1½-inch) florets broccoli
Freshly grated Parmigiano-Reggiano

Note: Make the lemon vinaigrette and pickled beet and red onion ahead. You can also make the capers ahead or right before serving, chef's choice.

To make the lemon vinaigrette: Mix the lemon juice and zest, mustard, garlic, thyme, and salt in a bowl with a whisk. Drip by drip add in the oils while whisking until an emulsion starts to form. Increase the stream and continue to whisk until oil is all incorporated.

To pickle the red onions: Put the vinegar, sugar, beet, and 1 cup water in a pot and bring to a boil. Pour over sliced onion and cover immediately. Let sit at room temperature for at least 8 hours, then refrigerate.

To fry the capers: Place the capers in a small pot and cover with canola oil. Turn up the heat and fry the capers until they are crispy. Strain the capers and place on a paper towel to dry. Reserve oil for another use, such as caper vinaigrette.

To make the warm winter salad: Using a benriner or mandoline, shred 5 brussels sprouts. Place in a large mixing bowl.

Remove thick ribs from the kale leaves, wash in cold water, dry, and slice into thin ribbons. Add to shredded brussel spouts.

Add pickled red onions to bowl.

Using the mandoline, slice the squash and carrots into long ribbons about ⅛ inch thick and 1 inch wide. Using the same thickness setting, cut round slices out of the parsnips. Toss with half the salt, half the pepper, and half the olive oil.

Cut the other 5 brussels sprouts into quarters. Toss the cauliflower, broccoli, and quartered brussels sprouts with remaining salt, pepper, and olive oil, and lay on a sheet tray. Roast under the broiler until starting to get some dark coloring, almost burning, at which point add the squash, carrots, and parsnips. When the root vegetables start to soften, after a couple of minutes, remove from the heat and toss with the shredded brussels sprouts and kale and onions. Add some of the dressing, and taste for seasoning.

To serve: Arrange the salad in a heaping stack and cover with freshly grated Parmesan and a sprinkling of the crunchy fried capers.

Seasonal Fruit & Rosemary Cobbler

(SERVES 6)

5 cups of seasonal fruit—strawberries, blueberries, peaches, or plums
1½ cups sugar
2 tablespoons cornstarch or tapioca starch
Zest and juice of 1 lemon
1 teaspoon vanilla
2 tablespoons heavy cream
¼ cup turbinado sugar or coarse sugar, for sprinkling

For the dough:

3 cups all-purpose flour
4 teaspoons baking powder
1 tablespoon sugar
1 teaspoon salt
1 tablespoon finely chopped fresh rosemary
12 ounces (3 sticks) cold unsalted butter
1½ cups heavy cream, well chilled

For the vanilla whipped cream:

1 cup heavy whipping cream, well chilled
2 tablespoons powdered sugar
Seeds scraped from ½ vanilla bean, or 1 teaspoon vanilla extract

First make the dough. In a small bowl, sift together the flour, baking powder, sugar, salt, and rosemary. Cut the butter into the flour, using a pastry cutter or two knives, until the butter is the size of small peas. Add 1½ cups chilled cream gradually, mixing with a wooden spoon or spatula, until a dough ball forms. Refrigerate the dough until ready to use.

Butter six 6-ounce ramekins or one large baking dish. If you are using stone fruits such as peaches or plums, peel and slice them about ¼ inch thick. If you are using strawberries, slice them in half. In a large bowl, mix the fruit with the sugar, starch, lemon zest and juice, and vanilla. Place the fruit mixture in the ramekins or baking dish.

Preheat oven to 350°F. Drop the dough on top of the fruit, making sure to spread it out so that it covers the fruit. With a pastry brush, brush the top of the dough with the heavy cream, and sprinkle with turbinado sugar. Place the ramekins or baking dish on a sheet tray. Bake for 30 to 35 minutes until the cobbler is golden brown. Let cool.

When ready to serve, prepare the whipped cream topping. In a cold bowl, whisk the cream, powdered sugar, and vanilla seeds or extract just until peaks form. Serve the cobbler warm with a dollop of the fresh whipped cream.

THREE MUSES

536 FRENCHMEN STREET
(504) 252-4801
THETHREEMUSES.COM
EXECUTIVE CHEF: DANIEL ESSES

Marigny hip with retro flair: that describes what is Three Muses. Opened in 2010 by the people "trinity" composed of Chef Dan Esses, jazz singer Sophie Lee, and general manager Christopher Starnes, known in "the industry" as Xtofer. Perfectly placed on hipper-than-hip Frenchmen Street, one of the city's musical hearts, Three Muses is a restaurant with great music and a club with great food and cocktails—it hits on all three cylinders. The restaurant-club interior is dark wood paneled, and the giant bar beckons patrons to kick off an evening with the house cocktail, the Muse: cucumbers, strawberries, St. Germain liqueur, and gin. Chef Daniel Esses's considerable background in white-tablecloth dining means food with a twist and an upscale sensibility. He is a craftsman and appreciates how to incorporate the flavors of Louisiana with ethnic, often Asian inspiration. His handmade pastas are often featured on the menu—he was once a vendor at the Tuesday Crescent City Farmers Market, selling those hand-rolled pastas and his sauces—as part of the vegetarian offerings. There is a lot to love on Dan's imaginative menu, from Steak & Cake (a quirky surf-and-turf that includes a crab cake), to crispy french fries tumbled with tangy feta and citrus-flecked gremolata, and even

the sometimes special of an eggroll larded with lobster. Everything at Three Muses is vivid, energetic, and busy. A wait for a table is fairly common, but no big thing, as Chris instructs: "I usually tell people to just relax, have a drink, a table will open soon." It's fine advice, allowing for time to be inspired by the Three Muses—music, food, and cocktails.

CIDER BRAISED PORK BELLY
OVER SCALLION PANCAKE

(SERVES 4 –6)

For the pork belly:

1 cup hard cider
½ cup chicken stock
½ cup light soy sauce
2 tablespoons oyster sauce
2 pounds pork belly, in a slab
2 tablespoons Louisiana honey
2 tablespoons vegetable oil

For the apple chutney:

4 tablespoons vegetable oil
1 small onion, minced
2 cooking apples, peeled and minced
1 piece star anise
3 coriander seeds
1 allspice berry
2 tablespoons sugar
2 tablespoons apple vinegar or apple cider vinegar
1 crisp eating apple, julienned, for garnish

For the scallion pancakes:

1 tablespoon vegetable oil
2½ cups flour
Pinch of salt
2 tablespoons toasted sesame oil
1 cup minced scallions, green part only
Vegetable oil for frying

To make the pork belly: Preheat oven to 325°F.

Mix cider, chicken stock, soy sauce, and oyster sauce in a bowl.

Place pork belly in a roasting pan. Pour sauce over pork belly. Cover with foil. Cook pork until knife goes through easily, about 1½ hours. Cool. Strain juices and reserve.

Remove pork to a sheet tray and cover with parchment paper. Place another sheet tray of the same size over the pork and weight with a brick or other heavy object. Allow to set overnight.

Meanwhile, combine reserved cooking liquid with honey and mix well.

Take cooled pork belly and slice it into three rectangular pieces. Cut each rectangular piece crosswise into 1-inch slices.

Heat a nonstick sauté pan with a little vegetable oil. Add a few pieces of belly at a time. Cook on each side until golden brown, then remove and reserve. Once all the pieces you want have been cooked crisp, add cooking liquid to pan and reduce by half. Set aside until serving time.

To make the chutney: Heat oil in a large pan set over medium-high heat. Add onion and cook until translucent, about 5 minutes. Add apple and cook until it begin to soften, again about 5 minutes. Stir in star anise, coriander, allspice, and sugar. Cook for 5 minutes until blended. Add vinegar. Cook until apples are soft, about 5 minutes more.

To make the pancakes: Place vegetable oil and 1 cup water in a small pot over high heat and bring to a boil. Cool for 5 minutes.

Mix flour and salt in a large bowl. Pour water and oil mixture over flour. Mix with a wooden spoon, then use your hands to mix well. Cover with plastic wrap and allow to cool.

Divide dough into six even pieces and flatten into 4-inch disks. Mix sesame oil, salt, and scallions. Roll the coated disks in the mixture, then form them into balls. Flatten each ball again into a disk.

To assemble: Heat vegetable oil in a pan set over medium-high heat until a drop of water sizzles in the oil, about 2 minutes. Fry the pancakes in batches until crispy. Drain on paper towels. Place a scallion pancake on each serving plate.

Meanwhile, reheat the reduced pork belly liquid, add back the pork belly, and just coat each piece. Place on scallion pancakes, top with apple chutney, and garnish with crisp apple juliennes.

Banana Mascarpone Strudel

(SERVES 8)

For the banana caramel sauce:

1 cup sugar
1 cup heavy cream
2 tablespoons Myers's rum
1 banana, diced

For the mascarpone strudel:

1 pound mascarpone
½ cup cream
1 cup sugar
2 bananas, diced
1 cup chocolate chips
½ cup crushed pistachios
6 ounces unsalted butter, divided
6 sheets phyllo dough

To make the sauce: In a saucepan over medium heat, cook sugar with 1 cup water until it turns to a medium-dark caramel. Add cream and whisk until totally incorporated. When you put the cream in, it will not look right, but leave it on medium heat and whisk and it will blend together. Add rum and stir. Let cook for 5 minutes, then add the banana and cook for 5 more minutes. Let cool.

To make the strudel: In the bowl of a stand mixer fitted with the whisk attachment, combine mascarpone, cream, and sugar. Whisk on medium until incorporated, just a few minutes. (You can do this by hand, but make sure to mix well.) On low speed now, add bananas, chocolate chips, and pistachios. Just mix to incorporate. Let cool in the refrigerator for 30 minutes.

Melt ½ cup (1 stick) butter. Take one sheet of phyllo and brush with melted butter, then put another sheet on top, brush it with butter, and do the same with a third sheet. Place a few spoonfuls of mascarpone banana mixture along the bottom of the phyllo. Roll into a long log, and cut log into four even pieces. Repeat the process with the remaining three sheets of phyllo. Place strudel pieces in freezer for 1 hour.

In a large nonstick pan, melt 2 tablespoons butter until it sizzles, add 4 pieces of strudel, and brown for about 30 seconds on each side. Repeat.

Serve with banana caramel sauce and your favorite ice cream. At our restaurant we use Mexican Chocolate.

FRENCH QUARTER

Bombay Club

830 Conti Street
(504) 586-0972
THEBOMBAYCLUB.COM
Executive Chef: Ricky Cheramie

Just off the bustle and buzz of Bourbon Street, tucked neatly inside the Prince Conti Hotel, is the Bombay Club. At first the place screams English pub; then there are the "cheater's booths" (curtain-draped booth tables), and white-clothed tables that are all clubby elegance. Tufted leather seating decks the lounge and music "stage" area and an uplit outdoor patio that is flanked by floor-to-ceiling glass. Richard and Willie Fiske have long and successfully run this outstanding cocktail lounge/pub/local music venue wrapped around a fabulous restaurant. The cuisine at Bombay Club has taken a few twists and turns over time, but there has always been a level of sophistication, giving the place a delicious dinner theatre vibration. The cocktail menu is massive and well known for the comprehensive martini list that bridges history and the contemporary cocktail movement. As for the food, Bombay Club is at the top of its game with Chef Ricky Cheramie, who came on board to helm the kitchen in 2011. He's a country guy gone city with a fine-dine background that lends itself well to the modern Louisiana fare he prepares with southern soul. Ricky loves to pull from his native roots, familiar flavors, and

local products, then ramp it up in style with dishes like Grilled Wild Louisiana White Shrimp with Andouille, Creole Sauce, Stone Ground Grits and Fried Okra Pickles, or a slow-roasted duck leg quarter served with grilled house-made boudin, slow-cooked greens and a sugarcane Creole mustard glaze. A don't-miss dish is Chef Ricky's Fried Oysters Rockefeller with Herbsaint-laced cream, bacon lardons, sautéed spinach, and roasted fennel. Big steaks, alligator étouffée and grits—the menu has everything. So does the Bombay Club, a gem hiding in plain sight.

Snapper Lafourche
(SERVES 4)

For the gratin:

12 mirlitons (chayotes)
1 tablespoon salt
2 tablespoons vegetable oil
1 cup chopped onions
½ cup chopped celery
½ cup chopped red and green bell peppers
1 bay leaf
1 tablespoon minced garlic
2 tablespoons Creole seasoning
1 cup chicken stock
1 pound stone crab meat (from claws)
2 tablespoons chopped scallion
1 tablespoon chopped parsley
2 cups panko bread crumbs
½ cup melted butter
2 tablespoons chopped fresh herbs of your choice

For the pepper jelly gastrique:

1 cup distilled vinegar
⅔ cup sugar
1 tablespoon red pepper flakes
½ teaspoon cayenne pepper
2 teaspoons minced jalapeño
Pinch of salt
1 tablespoon minced red bell pepper

For the fish:

4 red snapper portions, 6–8 ounces each
Kosher salt
Ground white pepper
4 tablespoons vegetable oil
2 tablespoons melted butter
½ cup chopped fresh herbs of your choice
1 tablespoon lemon zest

To make the gratin: Cut mirlitons in half. Bring 1 gallon water and 1 tablespoon salt to a boil. Add mirlitons and cook 12 to 15 minutes or until just fork tender; do not overcook. Cool mirlitons in an ice bath, remove seeds, peel, and dice. Set aside.

Heat a cast iron skillet or heavy-gauge pot on medium heat. Add oil. Saute onions, celery, and bell peppers for 3 to 5 minutes. Add bay leaf, garlic, and Creole seasoning. Cook an additional 3 minutes. Add mirlitons; cook 5 to 8 minutes, stirring constantly so mirlitons don't stick to the pot. Add ½ cup of the stock, and turn down heat to low. Continue cooking until mirlitons break down and look like stuffing, 30 to 40 minutes. Stir as needed. Add more stock if mixture becomes too dry or starts to stick. When mirlitons are done, fold in crab meat, scallions, and parsley. Remove from pot and set aside.

Place "mirliton stuffing" in a shallow baking dish. Mix bread crumbs, melted butter, and herbs. Top gratin with bread crumb mixture. Bake at 375°F for 15 to 20 minutes or to internal temperature of 165°F. (This gratin can be done up to 1 day ahead and refrigerated. To reheat, bake at 375°F for 20 to 25 minutes.)

To make the gastrique: Combine all ingredients except minced peppers in a small sauce pot over medium-high heat. Bring to a boil. Reduce heat to a simmer and reduce liquid by half. Add minced peppers and transfer to a cup to cool. (This can be done hours ahead and held at room temperature.)

To make the fish: Season the snapper with kosher salt and white pepper to your liking. Heat 2 tablespoons of vegetable oil in a cast iron skillet on medium-high heat. Cook the snapper, two pieces at a time, until slightly caramelized. Flip and cook about 30 seconds. Remove fish from heat and place in a shallow baking pan. Repeat process with the rest of the fish. Top the fish with butter, herbs, and lemon zest. (You may cook the fish to this point ahead of time.) Place the fish in a 425°F oven for 2 to 3 minutes or until cooked through. Serve immediately with gratin and gastrique served seperately on the side.

She-Crab Étouffée

(SERVES 4 AS ENTREE, 8 AS APPETIZER)

For the crab stock:

6 live female crabs
1 tablespoon vegetable oil
1 cup chopped onion
½ cup chopped celery
⅓ cup chopped carrots
1 bay leaf
½ teaspoon crab boil

For the roux:

1 cup vegetable or canola oil
¾ cup all-purpose flour
½ cup chopped onion
⅓ chopped bell pepper
1 cup chopped celery

For the étouffée:

2 tablespoons vegetable oil
2 cups chopped onions
1 cup chopped celery
1 cup chopped bell peppers
1 tablespoon minced garlic
1 bay leaf
1 tablespoon Chef Paul's Meat Magic
1 quart crab stock
1 cup dark roux
½–1 cup crab roe
½ teaspoon salt
½ teaspoon black pepper
1 pound jumbo lump crabmeat
2 tablespoons chopped scallion
1 tablespoon chopped parsley

To make the crab stock: Remove top shell from body, set aside orange roe (eggs) from top and body, remove gills from both sides, and break crab in half. In a medium-sized stockpot with vegetable oil, sauté vegetables over medium heat for 3 to 5 minutes. Add crab bodies and sauté an additional 3 minutes. Add 1½ quarts cold water, bay leaf, and crab boil. Reduce heat and simmer for about 45 minutes. Strain and set aside. (This can be done 1 to 2 days ahead of time.)

To make the roux: Heat oil in a cast iron or heavy-gauge pot over medium-high heat. Heat to the smoking point, about 375°F. Add flour, constantly stirring. Turn down heat to medium-low; continue stirring until roux is the color of milk chocolate. Add vegetables to stop the cooking process.

Remove from heat and cool. (Roux can be done ahead of time, and can be stored in the refrigerator for up to 2 weeks.)

To make the étouffée: Heat oil in a cast iron or heavy-gauge pot. Sauté onions, celery, and bell peppers over medium heat for about 5 minutes or until translucent. Add garlic, bay leaf, and Meat Magic; sauté 1 minute longer. Add crab stock. Bring to a boil, reduce heat, and simmer for 10 minutes. Add roux, half at a time, bringing to a boil after each addition. Reduce heat and simmer for 15 to 20 minutes. Add crab roe, salt, and pepper and simmer for 5 to 8 minutes or until roe is cooked through. Add crab meat, scallions, and parsley. Adjust seasoning to taste.

Serve with rice or fresh French bread.

GALATOIRE'S

209 BOURBON STREET
(504) 525-2021
GALATOIRES.COM
EXECUTIVE CHEF: MICHAEL SICHEL

One of the French Quarter's restaurant "grandes dames," Galatoire's has been in business since 1905. It is a place that has to be experienced as well as tasted for dishes that are shining examples of culinary history and yet manage to be relevant today. True French Creole cuisine, extraordinary service, and on the main dining floor a room with hum, buzz, and history. The spirit of Galatoire's remains blessedly unchanged—white tiled walls, checkered flooring, mirror-lined walls, servers dressed in tuxedos, an unparalleled atmosphere. There is nothing so glorious as spending a Friday afternoon lunch, lingering over cocktails, letting that turn into dinner. It is a New Orleans restaurant rite of passage. Among the more recent of Galatoire's brilliant additions, beyond opening the upstairs

rooms (where reservations are honored), was the relatively recent hiring of Executive Chef Michael Sichel. Galatoire's has long had great chefs running the kitchens, but Chef Michael brings something new and special to the situation. He is not a native New Orleanian, though his is a fully embedded transplant and much loved. He is effusive and genuine, talkative and smart, a front-and-center character breathing new life into Galatoire's—and he's massively talented. The food, for better, is what it is, old school. That said, there is a freshness that pops from those platters of soufflé potatoes, tangy shrimp remoulade, comforting Chicken Clemenceau, trout draped in lemony meunière sauce or beurre blanc, topped with lump crabmeat. It's all very familiar, some might even say fusty, but New Orleanians say, "Bring it on." Chef Michael honors tradition magnificently, thank you. And though some things have changed (ownership is a blend of old line and new guard), some things stay the same. Tradition #47: "Regulars just put it on their tab."

BROILED POMPANO WITH
LOUISIANA SHELLFISH STUFFING

(SERVES 10)

½ gallon milk

½ pound butter

2 cups flour

1½ cups Parmesan

1 cup sliced green onions

½ cup chopped parsley

1 cup bread crumbs

Salt, pepper, and cayenne to taste

½ pound crabmeat

½ pound cooked shrimp

½ pound crawfish tail meat

10 pompano fillets

¼ cup canola oil

In a medium pot, heat milk till warm. In a second pot, melt butter, then stir in flour and cook roux for 5 minutes on low heat, stirring with a wooden spoon; be careful not to brown. Pour the warm milk over the roux and whisk over a low heat for 45 minutes until roux is creamy, with no lumps, and the flour is cooked out. Stir in the Parmesan, green onions, and parsley. Once all the cheese is melted, fold in the bread crumbs. Season to taste with salt, pepper, and cayenne. Spread on a sheet tray to cool.

Fold crabmeat, shrimp, and crawfish meat into cheese sauce to complete your stuffing.

Butterfly the pompano fillets. In the middle place stuffing from tail to head and fold back the fillets to cover all but the center of the stuffing. Coat the fish lightly with oil.

Broil for 7 minutes, then finish in a 350°F oven for 4 minutes.

Soufflé

(SERVES 6)

For the pastry cream:

2 quarts milk
7 ounces sugar
1 teaspoon vanilla

For the liaison:

7 ounces sugar
8 egg yolks (separate the eggs and reserve the whites)
6¼ ounces flour

8 egg whites (from separated eggs)
1 tablespoon praline liqueur

For the crème anglaise:

½ quart cream
½ quart milk
1 teaspoon sugar, divided
13 egg yolks
1 teaspoon vanilla

To make pastry cream: Bring the three ingredients to a boil.

To cook liaison: combine and cook all three ingredients until thick. Let cool.

Whisk egg whites till soft peak/fold into pastry cream/add flavoring (in our case praline liqueur).

Sugar coat each ramekin and fill to the top. Place in 400°F oven until the soufflé rises.

To make the crème anglaise: Warm cream, milk, and half the sugar to a simmer. Whisk in yolks, vanilla, and second half teaspoon of sugar off heat. Let cool.

For serving: Break hole in the middle of soufflé with a spoon and pour crème anglaise inside.

GW Fins

808 Bienville Street
(504) 581-3467
GWFINS.COM
Executive Chef: Tenney Flynn

Chef-owner Tenney Flynn is a fish guru. He's the go-to guy when a weary food writer wants to know what's really happening in the industry. GW Fins is the brainchild of Chef Tenney and his business partner Gary Wollerman (GW), the restaurant's wine guru. Both have strong restaurant chops, and at Fins there are no dangling details. The broad, open room is classically appointed, contemporary but comfy. The bar area is small but mighty, with solid barkeeps putting out great cocktails with or without frills. Gary is in charge of the stunning, enormous, and award-winning wine list. The food at Fins is seafood-centric with a southern charm and sensibility. Chef Tenney credits the roots of his cooking style and acumen to his Georgia upbringing and soul food cook/teachers as well as his formal training. The truth is that while Fins is a fine-dining seafood restaurant, the biscuits that are everyone's first bite draw sighs of joy. Don't ask what makes them extra fabulous: it's lard. GW Fins sources seafood globally and locally, pulling from the world's waters so that diners can experience Alaskan king crab, bay scallops from the Northeast, snapper from the Gulf, bass from New Zealand, and even Louisiana stone crab claws. All the seafood is prepared simply and unmasked—no heavy sauces cover the works. Global

exploration is also tasted in the style and manner of preparation, as in the Asian-inflected recipe Chef Tenney has shared here. He is a selective about the seafood that comes in the door of his restaurant, printing a new menu every day to showcase the latest catch. It's not all fine-dine and fancy for Tenney—he and his crew love to be on-the-ground local participating in events in and out of the French Quarter, and their Fried Maine Lobster Po-Boy has taken first prize at the Oak Street Po-Boy Festival. Chef Tenney, on his rare day off, can be spotted dining around town. He's that guy, the one who patronizes fellow chefs' restaurants when he isn't in his own. "I love to see what everyone is doing, and I'm almost always impressed."

GW Fins Sautéed Louisiana Red Snapper with Mussels & Thai Curry Broth

(SERVES 4)

For the curry broth for mussels:

10 head-on U-15 shrimp
1 tablespoon olive oil
1 teaspoon diced ginger
1 shallot, diced
1 clove garlic, diced
1 kaffir lime leaf
3 basil stems, diced
2 tablespoons diced cilantro stems
1 lemongrass stalk, crushed and chopped
2 teaspoons green curry paste
2 cups shrimp stock
2 cans coconut milk

For the snapper with mussels:

2 pounds Maine or Prince Edward Island mussels
4 red snapper fillets, 7–8 ounces each, skin on
Salt and black pepper
Flour for dredging
2 tablespoons plus 1 teaspoon olive oil
2 tablespoons butter
¼ cup sliced chanterelles (optional)

1 link Chinese sausage, sliced thinly on the bias
Dash of fish sauce
5 cups curry broth for mussels
1 package fresh rice stick noodles
2 tablespoons chopped cilantro
2 tablespoons chopped Thai basil

To make the curry broth for mussels: Roughly chop the shrimp and sauté them in a little olive oil. Add the diced ginger, shallot, garlic, lime leaf, basil and cilantro stems, and lemongrass. Sweat-sauté for a few minutes on medium heat. Add the curry paste, and stir in the stock and 4 cups water. Cook at a low boil for 30 minutes. Add the coconut milk and return to a boil. Puree with an immersion blender and strain. Cool and refrigerate.

To cook the fish and soup: First, check mussels carefully to make sure they're alive. If open, gently squeeze the shells shut; if they're dead, the shell won't stay closed. Discard the dead ones.

Place four large pasta bowls in a warming oven.

Preheat 2 large, heavy sauté pans. Season the fillets on both sides with salt and pepper and dredge them in flour. Place 1 tablespoon olive oil and 1 tablespoon butter in each pan and place the fish in, two to a pan, skin side down. Cook 3 to 4 minutes and turn over.

Place 1 teaspoon olive oil in 4-quart pot and add the chanterelles and sliced sausage. Cook on medium heat stirring often for 2 minutes. Add the mussels and raise the heat. Cover and cook for 1 minute more. Add a dash or two of fish sauce.

Add the 5 cups curry broth and bring to a boil. Break the rice noodles into 4-inch pieces and add half the package to the boiling broth. Cook for 10 seconds, stirring so the noodles are immersed in the boiling stock. Add half the chopped herbs, and ladle the soup into the preheated pasta bowls.

Place a snapper fillet, skin side up, in the center of each bowl and garnish with additional Thai basil and cilantro.

IRIS

321 NORTH PETERS STREET
(504) 299-3944
IRISNEWORLEANS.COM
EXECUTIVE CHEF: IAN SCHNOEBELEN

Though it may embarrass the chef to death, there is a dead sexy picture of him from the June 2007 issue of *Food & Wine* magazine (when he was named one of their Top 10 Best New Chefs in America) that a certain food writer has taped to the inside of a notebook. Ian's good looks aside, he's an incredible culinary talent. Originally from Hawaii, Ian came to New Orleans in 1993 looking for adventure. Tapping into his cooking skills, he worked at a couple of New Orleans restaurants, helped open Commander's Palace Las Vegas, traveled Europe and cooked there to refine his skills, then returned to our city where he was sous-chef at Lilette. After four years he and his partner, Laurie Casebonne, decided to open their own restaurant, Iris, which almost immediately became a hit, and resulted in the aforementioned national magazine nod. Soon they needed a bigger space, and

they took over the chicly designed space inside the Bienville House Hotel. Ian's nature is easygoing, but his new American cuisine burns with passion and bears a definite California feel. There isn't a Saturday that Ian isn't spotted at the farmers market, stocking up on fresh vegetables, fruits, and other products to blend into dishes like baby octopus salad with wild arugula, fennel, and grapefruit, or veal short ribs with lacinato kale and grilled endive. There's always a top-quality protein coupled with a thoughtfully managed, seasonally relevant vegetable. Ian offers a bar menu of raw seafoods and "not so raw" items, many with an Asian flavor profile. The cocktails are always surprising and attention-getting concoctions that fold in herbs, juices, and syrups built from kitchen groceries. New Orleans has a large Asian community and a tropical feel that Ian appreciates and taps into, as he did for the recipes he's provided here. Keep all eyes peeled for Ian and Laurie's next project, a restaurant in Bywater that will have a rooftop garden.

Yellowfin Tuna with Fennel Salad & Galangal Vinaigrette

(SERVES 1–2)

1 (1-inch) galagal root

1⅓ cups canola–olive oil blend, divided

⅓ cup white wine vinegar

2 tablespoons New Mexican chile powder

12 ounces yellowfin tuna, trimmed into a 2 x 3-inch log

Kosher salt and coarsely ground black pepper

1 fennel bulb

3 radishes

1 baby cucumber

Sunflower sprouts or other interesting sprout mixture

For the vinaigrette, slice galagal root and crush with a mortar and pestle. Place in a pot with 1 cup of blended oil. Heat until warm. Let infuse for at least 1 hour or a full day. Strain and whisk with white wine vinegar.

Meanwhile warm ¼ cup of blended oil and pour onto New Mexican chile powder. Strain through a fine mesh strainer or cheesecloth.

Season tuna heavily with salt and pepper. Sear on all sides in a large, heavy, smoking-hot pan with a little vegetable oil, being careful not to overcook the tuna. Place on a cutting board.

Shave fennel, radishes, and cucumber using a mandoline (careful with your fingers!). Toss in a bowl with galangal vinaigrette and sprouts. Salt to taste. Slice tuna into 1-inch pieces and place on plates with fennel salad. Spoon galangal vinaigrette over the tuna, and the chile oil around the plate.

Kaffir Lime Panna Cotta with Tropical Fruit Salsa & Caramelized Banana

(SERVES 8)

For the panna cotta:

¼ teaspoon unflavored gelatin
3 Kaffir lime leaves
2 cups heavy cream
½ cup sugar
¼ cup goat yogurt
Cooking spray

For the fruit salsa:

1 mango
½ pineapple
Juice of 3 limes
¼ cup simple syrup

For the basil syrup:

½ cup Thai basil leaves
¼ cup corn syrup
¼ cup simple syrup

For the caramelized banana:

1 banana
2 tablespoons sugar

To make the panna cotta: Sprinkle gelatin onto 2 tablespoons water in a bowl. Crush Kaffir lime leaves with a mortar and pestle. Place crushed leaves in a pot with heavy cream and sugar. Bring almost to boiling, stirring to dissolve sugar. Let sleep for 15 minutes. Strain. Add hot liquid to gelatin, whisking to dissolve. Add yogurt. Pour into eight 4-ounce ramekins that have been oiled very lightly with cooking spray. Let chill for 24 hours.

To make the salsa: Peel the fruit and dice it small. Add lime juice and simple syrup. (To make simple syrup, combine equal parts water and sugar in a pot, heat to a boil, then cool.)

To make the basil syrup: Bring a large pot of water to a boil. Plunge basil leaves into boiling water. Using a spider strainer, pull leaves out and plunge into ice water. Remove, and squeeze out water. Place in blender with syrups. Blend for 1 minute.

To make the caramelized banana: Slice banana on the bias to ¼-inch thickness. Sprinkle with sugar and caramelize with a blowtorch or run under broiler.

To assemble: Unmold each panna cotta gently and onto a plate. Place a scoop of fruit salsa next to it. Spoon some basil syrup around plate. Place caramelized bananas on top of panna cotta. Be careful—the bananas will be very hot!

Restaurant R'evolution

777 Bienville Street
(504) 553-2277
revolutionnola.com
Executive Chefs: Rick Tramonto and John Folse
Chef de Cuisine: Christopher Lusk

Chefs John Folse and Rick Tramonto are a little bit country, and a little bit rock 'n' roll.
It's an intriguing partnership that had been in the making for a couple of years before
the doors to R'evolution finally swung open. After a lot of pomp and circumstance,
dollars spent and the build-out completed, the Royal Sonesta Hotel now boasts a
jaw-dropping multiroom restaurant evocative of a fine Creole mansion, complete with
culinary ephemera, historic knickknacks, and a tricked-out kitchen that's the envy of
every chef. Executing the gargantuan menu, Chef Chris Lusk brings his enormous talent
to turning out a wild bouquet of styles, flavors, and foods from old Louisiana and the
"seven nations" that are her composition—Italian, French, Spanish, German, Acadian,
and Native and African American. The restaurant serves breakfast, brunch, lunch,
and dinner of interpreted classics like gumbo and jambalaya, or corn and crab soup,
as well as a host of meats, charcuterie, pastas, and specialty items like the Triptych of
Pork (pork belly, smoked tail, and crispy ears) that is a head-to-tail tribute to Louisiana's
boucherie tradition. Seafood, vegetables, wild game, and some contemporary-style
sweets (chicory mocha pots de crème with coffee-infused beignets and black fig jam)

round out the menu and, of course, there is a gorgeous bar where top mixologists shake up reimagined vintage cocktails or pour out a local craft beer. Chef Chris has shared a dish that exemplifies our love for Louisiana's crustacean bounty and the spirit of New Orleans's Creole-Italian culinary heritage.

Fazzoletti & Crawfish Pasta

(SERVES 4)

For the crawfish stock (yields 4 cups):

1 pound crawfish heads
¼ cup roughly chopped onion
2 garlic cloves, crushed
2 tablespoons olive oil
3 lemons, thinly sliced
2 bay leaves
¼ teaspoon liquid crab boil
¾ teaspoon salt

For the fazzoletti pasta dough (yields 1 pound):

6 ounces bread flour
6¼ ounces all-purpose flour
4 eggs
1 tablespoon water

For the entree:

¼ cup crawfish stock
½ cup corn juice
2 tablespoons corn kernels
2 tablespoons olive oil
3 ounces crawfish tails
1 tablespoon butter
2 tablespoons grated Parmesan
Salt and freshly ground black pepper
3 ounces fazzoletti pasta, dry
2 fried sage leaves
Corn powder, for sprinkling
Grated orange zest, for sprinkling

To make the crawfish stock: Roast crawfish heads in a 350°F oven for 15 to 20 minutes. Sweat onions and garlic with a little olive oil until soft. Add remaining ingredients and 4 cups water. Simmer slowly for 20 minutes, skimming constantly. Strain.

To make the pasta: Combine ingredients in the bowl of electric mixer and mix for 5 minutes with the paddle. Wrap in plastic wrap and rest for one hour before use. Roll out using a pasta machine to number 2. Cut into 3 inch by 1½ inch rectangles.

To prepare the dish: In a large skillet, warm the crawfish stock, corn juice, corn, and olive oil. Cook corn until tender. Add the crawfish tails, butter, and Parmesan and bring to a boil, adding butter a bit at a time. Season lightly with salt and pepper to taste.

Cook pasta in boiling, salted water for 4 minutes or until tender.

Add the cooked pasta to the skillet and toss. Serve in a pasta bowl, and sprinkle the top with fried sage leaves, corn powder and orange zest.

SoBou

310 Chartres Street
(504) 552-4095
SOBOUNOLA.COM
Executive Chef: Juan Carlos Gonzalez

The newest "baby" of the Commander's Palace family of restaurants, SoBou is so named for its location south of Bourbon Street. "Cocktail Chicks" Ti Martin and Lally Brennan took over the space inside the W New Orleans French Quarter hotel that was once another Brennan family member's restaurant to create a "spirited restaurant." At first, the focal point appeared to be adult beverages, including automated wine dispensers, tableside beer taps, and a custom cocktail list from top bar gal Abigail Gullo (there is big love for her margarita dressed up with lavender syrup), but it is indeed a restaurant. Designed high style and modern with chic lighting fixtures and sleek details like row after row of apothecary bottles in clear and frosted glass that pack up-lit glass shelving, or a gorgeous marble-topped bar and wine menu covered in patinated copper—the feel is sharply cosmopolitan and new. Make no mistake, food at SoBou is in no way an afterthought or second fiddle. Executive Chef Juan Carlos Gonzalez demonstrates his culinary fire and passion throughout the menu, shoring up all the style and adding a welcome blend of tradition and modernity. Evidence the Cochon de Lait Gumbo, or the Sticky Pork Belly, molasses-lacquered and served with a Dirty Rice Calas. A petite jar of blue crab mousse is topped with beautiful ghost pepper–scented Louisiana caviar, to be scooped and dolloped atop house-made crackers. There are small cones filled with

tuna tartare and a wee scoop of basil and avocado ice cream, and nothing is more lavish than sipping a mini Abita Root Beer and Foie Gras Ice Cream Float while nibbling on a baby burger topped by a bit of seared foie lobe, a sunny-side-up fried duck egg, duck bacon, foie mayo, and all of it piled on a rich brioche bun. Chef Juan Carlos lets his Latin roots show via his version of Commander's Shrimp & Tasso Henican done at SoBou as pinchos—shrimp skewered and shooting tall from a base of grilled pineapple. The drink recipe is special to this book and heavenly, a Puerto Rican rum–spiked eggnog that is one of Juan Carlos's favorites.

Shrimp & Tasso Pinchos

(SERVES 8–10)

30–40 (7-inch) bamboo skewers
2 pounds 16/20-count white shrimp, peeled and deveined, tail on
1½ pounds tasso or substitute a good quality smoked ham, in large dice
Creole seasoning to taste

For the chimichurri rub (yields enough for 40 pinchos):

1 bunch flat-leaf parsley, roughly chopped
1 bunch cilantro, roughly chopped
3 ounces minced garlic
Juice of 3 lemons
1 ounce cane vinegar
16 ounces canola or vegetable oil
1 tablespoon Creole seasoning
1 teaspoon red pepper flakes
2 tablespoons salt
1 tablespoon black pepper
2 tablespoons Parmesan cheese

For the pineapple ceviche (yields 12 servings):

1½ pounds pineapple, diced
6 ounces red onion, diced
4 ounces piquillo pepper, diced
2 ounces green onion, thinly sliced
2 ounces cilantro, finely chopped
1 splash of Crystal hot sauce
Juice of 3 lemons
Juice of 2 limes
Juice of 1 orange
Salt and pepper to taste

For the pickled jalapeño pepper jelly (yields 2½ cups):

1 cup white vinegar
1 cup cane vinegar
2 cups light Karo syrup
½ cup finely chopped pickled jalapeños
2 teaspoons sea salt
1 teaspoon black pepper
1 teaspoon red pepper flakes
1 teaspoon smoked paprika

To make the chimichurri rub: In a food processor, combine all ingredients and blend to the consistency of a wet paste.

To make the pineapple ceviche: In a large mixing bowl, combine all ingredients, toss thoroughly, and allow to rest for 40 minutes.

To make the jelly: In a large pot combine all ingredients and cook on medium-low heat to the consistency of syrup. Set aside to cool to room temperature.

To make the pinchos: Take a skewer and carefully push through the shrimp, starting from the tail end. Then take a piece of tasso and add it to the skewer. Repeat until all the shrimp are skewered. Place the pinchos on a sheet pan. Rub them with the chimichurri and let them marinate for 30 minutes. Season the pinchos with Creole seasoning and cook on the grill until the shrimp is fully cooked, about 1½ minutes on each side.

On a serving tray place the pineapple ceviche in the middle. Arrange all the shrimp pinchos around the pineapple and drizzle them with the pickled jalapeño jelly. ¡Buen provecho!

COQUITO

PUERTO RICAN EGGNOG

(YIELDS ABOUT 2½ QUARTS)

30 ounces Coco López or cream of coconut
12 ounces evaporated milk
14 ounces sweetened condensed milk
22 ounces Don Q Crystal white rum
¼ tablespoon ground cinnamon
¼ tablespoon ground nutmeg
1 teaspoon vanilla extract

Mix all ingredients in a blender on high speed. Refrigerate. Make sure to shake well before serving. Serve cold, sip, and enjoy.

STANLEY

547 SAINT ANN STREET
(504) 587-0093
STANLEYRESTAURANT.COM
EXECUTIVE CHEF: SCOTT BOSWELL

When Chef Scott Boswell decides to pursue a project, he goes full force. Scott wanted to open a casual spot as counterpoint to his überelegant Restaurant Stella! He first launched the concept in a tiny coffee shop on Decatur, in the days immediately following the Hurricane Katrina flooding of the French Quarter. The food was manna—deep, dark seafood-and-sausage-studded gumbo, Eggs Benedict Poor Boys, fried oysters

or softshell crab with poached eggs, a tall bccfy Reuben, and the Stanley Burger he fed to reporters and first responders covering the disaster. When bigger digs were required, Scott tackled city and state politics and politicos, a big-box coffee corporation, and bank financing to garner and renovate a corner location on Jackson Square. He planned to continue serving his cheeky diner fare, expanding the menu to include a few specialty po-boys (bulgogi and house-made kimchi, for one) and added a soda shop component complete with ice cream, shakes, and malts. Then came fried chicken, a funny, boozy concoction he calls a Screamer and, and, and. Chef Scott knows no boundaries. This recipe for Stanley's Omelet Sandwich was among the menu favorites devoured by those who ate at the first Stanley on Decatur Street, during those strange, desolate days of late September 2005.

OMELET SANDWICH

(SERVES 1)

1 tablespoon butter, divided
1 ounce onions, sliced thick
1 ounce mayonnaise
Pinch of cayenne
2 ounces smoked ham, chopped
1 ounce bacon, chopped
½ ounce green onions, chopped
2–3 eggs
Salt and pepper to taste
2 slices American cheese
2 slices 9-grain bread

To caramelize the onions: On high heat, melt ½ tablespoon of butter in a nonstick frying pan. Add onions and stir frequently until golden brown. Set aside.

To make the spicy mayonnaise: Mix mayonnaise and cayenne pepper thoroughly.

To prepare the omelet: Melt ½ teaspoon of butter into a 6 inch, non-stick frying pan on medium heat. Add caramelized onions, smoked ham, chopped bacon and green onions and mix until all ingredients are coated in warmed butter.

Crack 2–3 eggs into bowl and add salt and pepper. Whisk vigorously. Add eggs to pan and gently stir until ingredients are evenly distributed. Allow to cook for about 1 minute, until the bottom of the eggs has set without coloring. With a heat-resistant rubber spatula, gently flip the omelet over and allow to cook for another 30 seconds, or until eggs are fully cooked. Fold omelet in half, add both slices of American cheese to top, and allow to melt in broiler.

To assemble: Brush butter on each side of 9-grain bread and toast, then add spicy mayonnaise to each slice. Once cheese has melted on omelet, place on bread and close the sandwich.

Stella!

1032 Chartres Street
(504) 587-0091
RESTAURANTSTELLA.COM
Executive Chef: Scott Boswell

Stella! is singular in New Orleans—there is no other restaurant like it and no other chef quite like Scott. Functioning as a sort of high-end culinary laboratory, Stella! is where Scott trots out his most intense and bold culinary expressions. Dining here is always a surprise and exceedingly elegant. The room is hushed and pretty, the tableware fine French porcelain, the service at one time white-gloved, though a recent dinner revealed the gloves have come off . . . on the servers and in Scott's latest concept. There is no a la carte menu, only a four-course menu (with options) and a seven-course fixed menu. The dishes are quintessential Boswell, calling for the finest-quality ingredients, sourced locally when possible, but not exclusively. His repertoire has no boundaries, his career is a continuing education—Scott does "stages" with world-class chefs like Grant Achatz, Charlie Trotter, Jean-Georges Vongerichten, and Scott's kindred spirit in auto racing as well as food, Daniel Boulud. Dining at Stella! is to expect feasting on the finest truffles from Alba, caviar from the Caspian Sea (Atchafalaya Basin too), imported giant prawns, or slow-braised Spanish octopus. There is Wagyu beef that appears on an individual brazier, accompanied by assorted fruit or vegetable kimchi, the famous Duck 5 Ways, and Chili Prawns that will likely be menu mainstays to avoid customer mutiny. Desserts have always been smart, sexy, and simple, the wines exceptional, the cocktails stirred and shaken well. Scott's belief in his culinary destiny keeps him changing and refreshing Stella!'s menu and style, often. New Orleans gets a kick out of Scott's eclectic endeavors to "create a culinary performance in everything he does," noting happily that many a passionate chef may have come from Louisiana's Cajun Country, but there is no one, no cook, quite as fascinating as Chef Scott Boswell.

Ricotta and Speck Agnolotti with English Peas & Porcini Mushroom Nage

(SERVES 1, MAY BE DOUBLED)

For the handmade pasta:

2 ounces semolina
2 ounces high-gluten flour
1 egg
1½ teaspoons extra virgin olive oil
⅓ teaspoon salt

For the filling:

1 cup ricotta cheese
½ cup chopped speck or cured Italian meat
Salt and pepper
Extra virgin olive oil to taste

For the broth:

15 button mushrooms

For the garnish:

5 porcini mushrooms
5 tablespoons butter
2½ teaspoons minced garlic
5 teaspoons chopped onion
Salt and pepper to taste
5 tablespoons English peas, shucked and blanched

To make the pasta: Blend all ingredients and knead dough thoroughly. Place dough in a large bowl and cover the bowl tightly with plastic wrap. Allow dough to cool in the refrigerator for 30 minutes.

To make the filling: Mix ricotta cheese and chopped meat. Add salt, pepper, and olive oil to taste.

To make the broth: Cook button mushrooms in 1 gallon water on low heat for 6 hours. Strain, then allow to reduce for 20 minutes.

To assemble: Use a rolling pin to create a thin sheet of pasta. Cut pasta sheet into a 12 x 4-inch rectangular shape. Using a piping bag, horizontally pipe ricotta filling along bottom ½ inch of pasta sheet. Fold from bottom to top about 1½ inches, and then fold again, creating a log shape. Portion the pasta log into 2-inch pieces and cook in a large pot of boiling salted water until pasta is cooked through and afloat.

To make the garnish: Remove dirt from porcini mushrooms, wash, and slice. Melt butter in a small sauté pan on high heat and add garlic, onions, porcini, and salt and pepper to taste.

To plate: Heat 2 ounces of broth and add peas and porcini mushrooms. Place pasta in a bowl and add broth with garnish.

A MUFFULETTA NAMED DESIRE

Mikko is a culture, theatre, and history buff who has shared a foodie version of Tennessee Williams's *A Streetcar Named Desire* reimagined by him and his fellow writer Lisa McCaffety. Beloved local chef Anthony Spizale, a local guy of Creole Italian heritage, makes some of the best olive salad and, in typical fashion, came up with a creative Muffuletta Hand Pie recipe to go along with Mikko and Lisa's "book."

A MODEST FRENCH QUARTER HOME.

There is a hubbub of four men, Stanley, Mitch, Pablo, and Steve, and a woman, Stella, scurrying around the kitchen. They are all preparing food for an upcoming affair. Stella moves with an unassuming flair that threatens neither women nor the men that want to be women. Stanley chops olives with a virility rarely seen in the musky, husky vapors of the swamps commonly found around the decaying and decadent crescent that is the city known as New Orleans. The other men are not attractive to me; I will say a few more things about Stanley: He is carnal in his manners, there is the touch of the animal in him as if any moment he will prepare a country-style gazpacho and not use any oregano. His leering, muscular innuendo propels the project in the kitchen—women and men around him sense the audacity of his Viking-like chopping. He— Excuse me? Well, I am starting the play . . . Pardon? This is necessary for me to lay the scene . . . What? . . . Do you know I am friends with Liz Taylor and Anna Magnani? . . . But Paul Newman said . . . Oh very well! (Sigh) . . .

Polka music plays in the background. . . . Bitch.

STANLEY   Hey Stella!
STELLA   Whatcha yellin' for, Stanley? I'm right here.
STANLEY   Meat!

Throws a packet of deli meat to her, but she is so close it sails over her head and crashes into the spice rack.

MITCH   Hey Stanley, how do you convert from teaspoons to metric?
STANLEY   Whatcha lookin' at metric for? What are ya, some kind of swishy lavender European?
MITCH   What's wrong with European? That's the old country, ain't it?
STANLEY   Look, can it. My family came to America to be in America. This is the land of the free. And you, Pablo, put down those carrots, I ain't lettin' no beaner touch my olive salad.

During this exchange, a slight but radiant woman enters unseen. She is shy, but with a trace of coquettishness that is attractive only when found in wispy females that portend or pretend nobility. There is the sense of a moth about her, as if she would dash herself to perdition against the dangerous lightbulbs of society's useless mores. She might even be mistaken for a butterfly and in certain parts of the world, even this rutting and rotting village in the marshes of the Mississippi delta, a delicate hummingbird that passes from sweet and forbidden flower to another damning— Pardon? I would remind you that Gore Vidal once confided in me . . . Who is Gore Vidal? Now, Truman, you are crossing the line . . . but . . . but . . . (Sigh) Fine.

The polka music settles into a plaintive tuba in a minor key.

BLANCHE   I was told to take a streetcar named "Desire" then transfer to the "Cemeteries" bus and then get off at Elysian Fields.
STANLEY   (Barking at her) It ain't a streetcar no more.
BLANCHE   Oh, I apologize, I . . .
MITCH   *(Soothingly approaches her.)* That's all right, Ma'am. He means that "Desire" is a bus now, not a streetcar.
BLANCHE   That explains my forty-seven-block promenade from the Greyhound station.
MITCH   *(Smiling)* You sure don't look like you walked forty-seven blocks.
STANLEY   Mitch! Get over here and chop this celery!
BLANCHE   Oh, you are a chef de cuisine?
MITCH   Nah, we all just get together and make New Orleans specialties.
STANLEY   *(Coming over with a bunch of celery, interrupting.)* I'm gonna make a special New Orleans punch on the side of your head if you don't get over to that chopping board.

He tosses the bunch of celery back to the work area in the kitchen, where it smashes into a group of empty beer bottles on top of the refrigerator.

You must be Stella's big sister.

BLANCHE   *(Her retiring demeanor drops and she embodies a beaming charm.)* Younger sister, actually, but I forgive you, for my sister eternally channels the vitality and allure of Aphrodite.
STANLEY   Mm-hmm. What do you think about canola oil?

(continued on page 144)

MUFFULETTA HAND PIE

(MAKES 20 HAND PIES)

4 ounces mortadella

4 ounces Genoa salami

4 ounces prosciutto

1 pound provolone

2 ounces grated Parmigiano-Reggiano

1 cup plus 1 tablespoon extra virgin olive oil

½ cup green olives, pitted

½ cup kalamata or other black olives, pitted

2 ounces capers

1 celery rib, thinly sliced

1 teaspoon garlic, finely chopped

1 small carrot, peeled and diced

1 roasted red pepper, diced

1 bunch green onions, sliced

3 tablespoons red wine vinegar

2 tablespoons dried oregano

6 fresh basil leaves, torn

1 teaspoon Italian parsley, finely chopped

1 teaspoon crushed red pepper flakes

Kosher salt and freshly ground pepper, to taste

1 (14-ounce) package dough disks for empanadas

Vegetable oil, for frying

2 ounces sesame seeds

Cut the three meats and the provolone in small dice. Toss in a bowl with the grated Parmigiano-Reggiano and 1 tablespoon olive oil. Set aside.

Combine green olives, black olives, and capers in a large stainless steel bowl. Crush the olives and capers with your hands. Add the celery, garlic, carrots, roasted peppers, and green onions. Toss together lightly.

Combine red wine vinegar with 1 cup olive oil, dried oregano, basil, parsley, and red pepper flakes. Season to taste with salt and pepper. Blend well. Add to the meat-cheese mixture and toss together lightly with the olive salad. Cover and refrigerate 2 to 3 hours.

Lay out empanada disks on a floured work table. Spoon about 1 tablespoon of meat and olive mixture into the middle of one disk. Fold in half to form a half moon; moisten edges with water and pinch to close, or seal with a fork. Repeat for the rest of the dough disks.

Fill a deep saucepan with oil to a depth of 2½ inches. Heat oil over medium-high heat until hot but not smoking, 350°F on deep-fry thermometer. Cook empanadas in batches, flipping once, until crisp and golden brown, 4 to 6 minutes. Transfer to paper towels to drain, and sprinkle with sesame seeds.

BLANCHE   Oh, Mr. Kowalski, I disdain it. And except for that Italian elixir from the fruit of the olive tree, I eschew all oils as I would a crass remark or a vulgar gesture.

STANLEY   STELLA!

BLANCHE   (This ejaculation has unnerved her. She reaches into her purse for a cigarette.) Yes, where is my lovely sister?

STANLEY   (Indicating her purse.) You got any Vidalia onions in there?

BLANCHE   Why, no . . .

STELLA   (Entering.) Oh, Blanche, my darling baby, how was your trip? I'm so glad to see you. I hope Stanley has been making you feel welcome.

Stanley grunts, and goes back to his work.

STELLA   Let's go in the other room and catch up.

They enter another part of the house where Blanche starts to unpack her things.

STELLA   Would you like a nice lemon Coke to cool you down, baby?

BLANCHE   Oh, my angelic sister, as the poet said, "My soul thirsteth . . ."

Stella goes back into the kitchen to prepare the drink. Stanley pulls her aside. Blanche turns the television on. The polka music becomes accusatory and insinuating.

STANLEY   Listen, baby, you think she brought any with her?

STELLA   Any what? Honest to God, Stanley, the poor girl has had a hard trip and you want to bother her with silly things.

STANLEY   It ain't so silly. What they got here in Louisiana is what you call your Muffuletta Code. In the Muffuletta Code it says that Vidalia onions are the best for a great olive salad. Vidalia onions grow best in Mississippi, and your sister is from Mississippi.
            (To Blanche in the other room.) Quiet down that racket!

STELLA   You know, Stanley, you should pay more attention to your salami.

She returns to her sister with the drink.

MITCH   Your sister-in-law is a charming girl.

STANLEY   Listen, I got an acquaintance friend of mine that is a salesman. He has occasion to travel through Laurel, Mississippi, a lot, and he tells me there is this blonde fancy-pants that is known as the Vidalia Queen.

MITCH   (Getting angry) Now just stop right there! You don't know everything, you know!

Mitch storms out of the kitchen into the dark and uncertain night.

STANLEY   (To the ladies in the other room.) You two cut out that racket!

He storms into the other room. The two ladies are watching Emeril on TV. We hear Emeril:

EMERIL (O.S.) . . . Sprinkle a few jimmies on the chocolate and Bam! (Or whatever it is Emeril says) we got a delicious doughnut! (We hear the audience clapping) Now that my friends, is a doughnut! . . .

STANLEY   (Throwing the TV out of the window.) Cut the re-bop!

Stella is so upset she storms out of the room into the disquieting safety of night.

BLANCHE   (Frightened.) I am not afraid of you.

STANLEY   (Approaching her) What we got here in Louisiana is the Muffuletta Code . . .

BLANCHE   I don't know your brand of Italian, Mr. Kowalski, the only Italian I know is the strains of Verdi, Puccini . . .

Stanley grabs her purse and tears it apart. As he continues to root through her many bags, she dissolves into that state that many true artists and very few people who have not lived in the French Quarter understand.

BLANCHE   Puccini, that's right. Tosca, who is set upon by the beast of a man Scarpia. She pleads with him, in the way I plead with you. Vissi d'Arte! Vissi d'arte!

Stanley has found a travel bag, and as he rips the zipper open, dozens of Vidalia onions tumble out onto the floor. Blanche swoons to the daybed.

BLANCHE   (continued) Yes! I have lived for art! Yes! I have lived for Vidalia onions!

Blanche collapses spent to the couch. Stanley drops to his knees in ecstasy, throwing the Vidalia onions into the air above him. He rejoices. The polka shifts into a somber indictment of masculinity.

STANLEY   Stella! Stella!!! HEY, STELLA!!!!!

Curtain.

Sylvain

625 Chartres Street
(504) 265-8123
SYLVAINNOLA.COM
Executive Chef: Alex Harrell

In a space that was once a fabulous French bakery just off Jackson Square, Sylvain is a dark, pubby sort of place, all dark wood, leather-topped stools, and low lighting. Take the narrow walkway onto the courtyard where the slave-quarter-housed kitchen is immediately visible. A sharp left through the French doors leads to the hostess station and bar and, just beyond that, a handful of tables that face Chartres Street. Owner Sean McCusker, an entrepreneur and occasional travel/food writer, dived headfirst into the restaurant industry with a menu of crafty cocktails stirred by dedicated mixologists, and even craftier food by a clean-cut southerner, Executive Chef Alex Harrell. Alex sources and cooks with an intensity that belies his low-key, almost shy nature. It's a brilliant combination reflected in food that surprises with depth and simplicity. Welcome to the French Quarter's brawniest yet most elegant gastropub. Harrell has grits milled to spec from his wife's Alabama hometown of Coosa Valley and, fancying pickled vegetables, has a varied and rotating selection of the season's harvest all distinctively brined and spiced. Braised Italian sausage with polenta and stewed eggplant is big shouldered, whereas the Chick-Syl-vain expresses southern fried humor. This is a marriage of history and modernity that works beautifully and has undeniable longevity.

Pickled Gulf Shrimp with Local Tomatoes, Butter Beans, Sprouts & Green Goddess Dressing

(SERVES 4 AS APPETIZER, 2 AS ENTREE)

For the shrimp boil:

1 teaspoon yellow mustard seeds

1 teaspoon coriander seeds

3 bay leaves

1 teaspoon whole black peppercorns

1 teaspoon red pepper flakes

1 lemon, cut in half

½ tablespoon white wine vinegar

4 whole garlic cloves, crushed

1 tablespoon sea salt or kosher salt

For the pickled Gulf shrimp:

1 pound Gulf shrimp

2 quarts shrimp boil

1 cup extra virgin olive oil

¼ cup freshly squeezed lemon juice

1 medium yellow onion, thinly sliced

4 crushed garlic cloves

½ teaspoon ground celery seeds

½ teaspoon red pepper flakes

½ teaspoon yellow mustard seeds

½ teaspoon coriander seeds

6 bay leaves

For the Green Goddess Dressing:

1 teaspoon chopped anchovies

1 tablespoon chopped chives

1 tablespoon chopped tarragon

½ tablespoon chopped basil

¼ cup chopped flat-leaf parsley

½ teaspoon minced garlic

½ cup mayonnaise

¼ cup buttermilk

1 teaspoon lemon juice

1 tablespoon apple cider vinegar

Pinch of kosher salt

Black pepper to taste

For the salad:

1 pound pickled Gulf shrimp

2 ripe tomatoes, sliced

1 cup butter beans, blanched in salted water

1 ounce sprouts—sunflower, pea, radish

Salt and pepper

½ tablespoon extra virgin olive oil

6 ounces Green Goddess Dressing

To make the shrimp boil: Combine all ingredients in a large sauce pot with 2 quarts water and bring to a boil over medium-high heat. Reduce the heat and simmer the liquid for 5 minutes.

To make the pickled Gulf shrimp: Cook the shrimp in the boil until they have started to turn pink, about 2 minutes. Place the oil, lemon juice, onion, garlic, and herbs and spices in a mixing bowl and whisk to combine. Toss the shrimp with this pickling mixture and place in a nonreactive container. Refrigerate for at least 1 hour before serving. The shrimp will keep for 3 days under refrigeration.

To make the Green Goddess Dressing: Place all the ingredients in a food processor or blender and process until smooth and green, about 30 seconds. Adjust salt and pepper to taste.

To make the salad: Toss the pickled Gulf shrimp, tomatoes, butter beans, and sprouts with salt, pepper, and extra virgin olive oil. Divide half of the Green Goddess Dressing between 2 or 4 plates. Place even amounts of shrimp and tomato mixture on the plates. Drizzle the plates with the remaining Green Goddess Dressing.

DOWNTOWN
&
CBD

Bittersweet Confections

725 Magazine Street
(504) 523-2626
BITTERSWEETCONFECTIONS.COM
Executive Chef: Cheryl Scripter

New Orleans first tasted Cheryl Scripter's nobby handmade chocolate truffles when she rolled them out at the Crescent City Farmers Market in 2001—deep, dark high quality, sometimes left plain, sometimes flavored with essences or spices and then tumbled in cocoa powder, bright fruit powders, or crisp croquantes. Cheryl tutored sweets eaters in the art of chocolate, and the city was addicted. Evolving her chocolate selection to include special collections with a local beat, Bittersweet Confections literally melted hearts. Suddenly there were more confections, cakes, chocolate-dipped fruits, and a slew of lovely chocolaty treats. Cheryl's first shop on Canal Boulevard succumbed to Hurricane Katrina, and it was only a scant year ago that she was able to reopen her business, this time in more highly foot-trafficked downtown New Orleans. Cheryl and her baking, confection-making crew continue to truffle, but they also fashion nonpareils, dip caramels, and cluster coconut in chocolate. They bake big, delectable King Cakes, fun-flavored cupcakes, killer cookies, chewy brownies; the list is endless. In short, there is a bit of chocolate confection heaven right here in the Crescent City, and it's Bittersweet . . . for those minding their waistlines.

Bittersweet Confection Marshmallows

(YIELDS 32 MARSHMALLOWS)

2¼ cups 10X sugar

2¼ cups cornstarch

Nonstick cooking spray

4½ cups granulated sugar

1½ cups white corn syrup

2¼ cups cold water

¾ teaspoon salt

1½ ounces gelatin

3 tablespoons pure vanilla extract

10 ounces 58% chocolate

4 ounces graham crackers

Sift the 10X sugar with the cornstarch into a small bowl. Spray two 9 x 9 x 2-inch baking pans with nonstick spray and coat with ⅓ cup of the powdered sugar–cornstarch mixture. Set aside.

In a medium heavy-bottomed pot, stir together the granulated sugar, corn syrup, 1½ cups water, and the salt. Bring to a boil over medium to medium-high heat and continue to cook until the temperature reaches 236°F.

Meanwhile, fill a medium bowl with remaining water and add ice. When syrup mixture reaches 236°F, remove the syrup pan from the heat and dip the bottom in the ice water for about 5 seconds to lower the temperature.

While waiting for the syrup to cool, put gelatin into the work-bowl of a stand mixer. When the syrup is down to 210°F, pour it into the gelatin and stir to combine. Mix at medium-high speed for 5 to 7 minutes, or until thick and fluffy. Add the vanilla and whip for another 30 seconds.

Spray a spatula with nonstick spray and scrape the marshmallow cream into the prepared pans. Sprinkle the remaining 10X-sugar-and-cornstarch mixture over the top of the cream. Let stand overnight.

Cut into squares. Temper 10 ounces of chocolate and finely crush 4 ounces of graham crackers. Dip each square into the chocolate and roll in the crumbs.

Borgne

601 Loyola Avenue
(504) 613-3860
BORGNERESTAURANT.COM
Executive Chef: Brian Landry

When Hyatt restored their hotel and created a restaurant space, they sought John Besh to consult on a seafood-based restaurant. Chef Besh partnered with a fellow native, chef, and avid fisherman (both liked to fish from Lake Borgne), Brian Landry. Landry, who'd been functioning as a chef and spokesperson for Louisiana's seafood industry in the wake of the Deep Water Horizon oil spill, had also spent five years as executive chef of legendary Galatoire's. Open to a new restaurant project, Brian came on board to help create Borgne, and as part of his research he traveled to the Canary Islands to learn about the Isleño people, culture, and food that influence the dishes at Borgne. Lightly fried crabmeat croquettes, or buttery broiled or raw oysters (in season), may kick off a meal. Then there is the Fish in a Bag, a less elegantly named en papillote treatment of fish baked with sliced fennel, onions, and crab fat. That's right, crab fat. The oyster spaghetti is creamy and briny at once, and the stuffed whole flounder is a popular throwback favorite. Though seafood is the centerpiece, there are great pork-centric sandwiches, and meaty lunch specials that are New Orleans standards done anew. Buttery, garlicky shrimp is as essential as it gets. Imagine this sauce atop creamy grits or al dente pasta, or straight from the pan, the sauce sopped up by gorgeous New Orleans French bread . . . Hungry?

GARLIC CLOVE SHRIMP SAUCE

(SMALL BATCH SERVES 4–6)

5 pounds 10/15-count Louisiana shrimp

3 tablespoons Creole seasoning

¼ cup minced garlic

1 shallot, minced

1 cup plus 2 tablespoons extra virgin olive oil

¼ cup minced piquillo peppers

½ teaspoon red chili flakes

½ tablespoon kosher salt

½ tablespoon sugar

1 cup dry sherry

3 tablespoons pure (not extra virgin) olive oil

Peel and devein the shrimp, leaving the tail on. Season the shrimp with 3 tablespoons of Creole seasoning and place in refrigerator. Place the shrimp shells in a 1½-quart saucepan, cover with water, and bring to a simmer. Allow shells to simmer for 30 to 45 minutes. Strain the stock from the shells. Measure out 1 quart for the sauce.

In a separate 2-quart saucepan, sweat the garlic and shallot in 2 tablespoons extra virgin olive oil for 2–3 minutes or until aromatic. Add piquillo peppers, chili flakes, salt, sugar, and sherry. Allow contents to come to a boil and reduce by half.

Add the shrimp stock and 1 cup extra virgin olive oil to pot and allow contents to simmer for 10 to 12 minutes or until all flavors have had a chance to mesh.

Heat 3 tablespoons pure olive oil in a cast iron skillet over medium-high heat. In small batches sear the shrimp on both sides until golden brown and just cooked through. Be careful not to overcook. Turn off the heat. Return all of the shrimp to the skillet and pour the garlic shrimp sauce over them. Garnish with fried garlic chips if desired.

CAFÉ ADELAIDE

300 POYDRAS STREET
(504) 595-3305
CAFEADELAIDE.COM
EXECUTIVE CHEF: CHRISTOPHER BARBATO

Often referred to as the sister restaurant of Commander's Palace, Café Adelaide opened as a more casual, bistro-esque restaurant than its fancier "sister." The walls were decorated to resemble wood planks, lighting sconces are sculptured pods of okra, and the menu is a collection of sassy New Orleans Creole dishes. The menu has gone through a few changes since its inception, and at present offers the smart and straightforward dishes of Executive Chef Chris Barbato. Chris earned his stripes as second-in-command to Chef Tory McPhail at Commander's Palace, and when Chris was offered the opportunity to shape the next iteration of Café Adelaide, he not only said "yes," he had a plan in mind. He loved much of what was already in place on the menu but wanted to streamline the flavors, simplifying the cuisine. Chris's efforts are a success. The 25-cent martini lunch is a blast for obvious reasons. Happy imbibers know that the cocktails at Café Adelaide come from "bar chef maestro" Lu Brow at Swizzle Stick, the attached cocktail emporium. At any time, any meal, order the Shrimp & Tasso "Corndogs" to start. Then, at lunch or brunch, dive face-first into a magnificent Croque Madame of shaved ham, béchamel sauce, heady Gruyère, Creole mustard, and a

sunny-side-up duck egg; never fear, there is a petite salad of baby greens tossed in a satsuma-fennel vinaigrette alongside. The Thursday lunch special of Crispy Oyster Tacos with slaw and tart tomatillo salsa is perfection. Dinner is lovely for the Tasso Pork Chop lacquered in rye whiskey and served with bacon smashed potatoes and a Creole mustard jus—luscious, bold, aromatic, smoky, tart, and sweet—or Chef Chris's Shrimp Courtbouillon, saffron-crusted Louisiana Gulf shrimp in an herbaceous green tomato sauce over creamy grits with a drizzle of saffron aioli and curls of Parmesan. Save room for dessert: Lemon Icebox Pie is de rigueur in New Orleans. Chef Chris uses locally grown Meyer lemons for the curd, pours it into a brown butter tart shell, and tops it with "burnt" marshmallows. Feel the urge to make this at home? See below.

Louisiana White Shrimp with Stone Ground Grits & Green Tomato Court Bouillon

(SERVES 6–8)

For the court bouillon:

8 ounces butter
3 garlic cloves, minced
1 medium yellow onion, diced
2 stalks celery, diced
1 each red, yellow, and green bell pepper, diced
3 bay leaves
1 teaspoon saffron
½ cup flour
2 green tomatoes, diced
2 cups white wine
2–3 cups fish stock
2 tablespoons each chopped thyme, parsley, and basil
2 tablespoons cane vinegar
Salt and pepper to taste

For the grits:

4 ounces butter
1 small shallot, diced
1 medium onion, diced
2 cups milk
1 cup seafood stock or water
1 cup stone ground grits
½ cup grated Parmesan
Salt and pepper to taste

For the shrimp:

¼ cup vegetable oil
30–35 9/10-count shrimp
Salt and pepper

To plate:

2 tablespoons grated Parmesan
3 tablespoons basil cut into ribbons (chiffonade)

To prepare the court bouillon: In a medium pot melt the butter over medium-high heat. Add garlic, onion, celery, peppers, bay leaves, and half of the saffron, and cook just until the onion begins to soften, approximately 4 to 8 minutes. Add flour all at once and stir vigorously, making sure there are no lumps. Add tomatoes, wine, and fish stock, bring to a boil, then lower to a simmer. Cook about 15 to 25 minutes, removing any foam with a ladle or spoon. Add remaining saffron, herbs, and cane vinegar and cook another 5 minutes. Season with salt and pepper at the end. If too tart because of really hard green tomatoes, you may add a little sugar also. Cool and store for up to 3 days, or hold hot and use upon serving.

To make the grits: In a medium pot over medium heat, melt butter. Add shallot and onion, and cook until onion is translucent. Add milk and stock, bring to a boil, and stir in grits vigorously to avoid lumping. Bring heat to low and cook grits for 35 to 45 minutes. Grits should be smooth, creamy, and tender. Stir in Parmesan, then adjust seasoning with salt and pepper. Hold hot until ready to use.

To make the shrimp: Place a large sauté pan over high heat and add oil. Bring the oil to the point where it is almost smoking, then add shrimp that have been seasoned with salt and pepper. Cook the shrimp about 2 minutes on each side. You will need to cook the shrimp in two separate batches. Remove the shrimp and place on a paper towel to absorb any extra grease. Do not overcook shrimp; medium-well to just well is fine.

To plate: Place about 1 cup of hot grits in the center of each large bowl. Ladle 6 to 8 ounces of hot court-bouillon sauce over grits. Place 4 to 5 shrimp on grits, then garnish with a little grated Parmesan cheese and chiffonade of basil.

Meyer Lemon Tart with Brown Butter Crust & Burnt Marshmallows

(MAKES A 9-INCH PIE)

For the marshmallows:

2 cups cornstarch
¼ teaspoon salt
2 cups powdered sugar
Cooking spray
3 tablespoons unflavored powdered gelatin
2 cups granulated sugar
2 tablespoons vanilla extract

For the Meyer lemon curd:

6 large eggs
6 large egg yolks
¾ cup sugar
1¼ cups Meyer lemon juice
¾ stick unsalted butter
2 tablespoons Meyer lemon zest, finely chopped

For the crust:

1 cup butter
½ cup powdered sugar
2 cups flour
¼ teaspoon baking powder

To make marshmallows: Combine cornstarch, salt, and powdered sugar, mixing well. Set aside.

Spray a regular-sized 8 x 8-inch square baking pan with cooking spray, line with plastic wrap, and spray again. Completely cover the inside of the sprayed pan with some of the cornstarch–powdered sugar mixture and shake excess back into the bowl.

Put ½ cup cold water and the gelatin into a mixer bowl and let stand for 10 to 15 minutes to bloom.

Combine 2 cups of granulated sugar and ¼ cup water in a pan. Cook until the mixture reaches soft-ball stage, 244°F.

Start mixer with whip attachment and slowly begin to add the boiling sugar syrup into the gelatin. Whip on high speed for about 20 minutes.

At the end, add vanilla extract and transfer mixture into lined pan. The mixture will be thick, creamy, and very white. Allow to cool for at least 4 hours.

Turn marshmallow mixture out onto a cutting board covered with some of the cornstarch–powdered sugar mixture. Take a pizza cutter, knife, or cookie cutter and cut out desired shape and size. Make sure that cutters are coated in cornstarch–powdered sugar mixture to prevent sticking.

Generously coat cut marshmallows with cornstarch–powdered sugar, shake off excess, and store in a single layer in an airtight container.

To make lemon curd: Combine eggs, yolks, sugar, and lemon juice, and whisk over a double boiler until the mixture reaches a temperature of 170°F. Strain mixture, then add butter and zest and whisk until creamy and emulsified. Cover and chill.

To make crust: Brown the butter in a small sauté pan (don't burn), strain, and chill.

Cream the brown butter and sugar together until light and fluffy. Sift flour with baking powder, then blend with butter-sugar mixture. Do not overmix.

Press crust into a 12-inch tart pan, chill 10 to 15 minutes until firm, then bake at 350°F for 12 to 15 minutes until the edges begin to brown

To assemble: Fill the prebaked shortbread crust with the lemon curd and bake at 350°F for about 5 minutes. This will help to smooth the top. Chill tart and cut into 8 to 12 pieces. Place a piece on each dessert plate and set a marshmallow on top. Be sure excess cornstarch–powdered sugar mixture is shaken off. With a handheld butane torch, brown the marshmallow on top of the tart to your taste.

Capdeville

520 Capdeville Street
(504) 371-5161
CAPDEVILLENOLA.COM
Executive Chef: James Eustis

In the winter of 2010, New Orleans had a rush of gastropubs, led by Capdeville. Directly across from Lafayette Square on Capdeville Street, owners Robert LeBlanc, Matt Alleman, and partner-general manager James Eustis created a cool social gathering space with kitschy Flavor Paper wall covering, black and white photography, '80s music on the jukebox, and a sharply run bar. Menu stars include a list of burgers, fries with a neat selections of toppings (manchego and chorizo is a standout), and a dreamy club sandwich of duck confit, cracklin's, and roasted garlic aioli. Red beans and rice are done as fried rounds to dunk in green onion aioli and reduced hot sauce, and, capitalizing on a trend with real sticking power, their Truffled Mac and Cheese with Brown Butter, Sage Pancetta, and Peas set the bar for all others and is perfect paired with a cold pint of locally brewed draft beer.

TRUFFLED MAC & CHEESE

(SERVES 4)

3 ounces pancetta

6 tablespoons unsalted butter

2 ounces fresh garlic, chopped

2 ounces fresh shallots, chopped

1 tablespoon fresh thyme

1½ ounces fresh sage, chopped

Salt and pepper

4 ounces heavy cream

3 ounces shredded Parmesan

8 ounces cooked elbow macaroni

1–2 ounces green peas

½ ounce white truffle oil

Fried sage leaves, for garnish

Shaved Parmesan, for garnish

Render pancetta (we use Molinari) in unsalted butter. As butter begins to brown, add garlic, shallots, thyme, sage, and a pinch of salt and pepper. As those ingredients combine, add the heavy cream and 2 ounces of the shredded Parmesan. Bring just to a boil and add cooked elbow macaroni. Continue to heat and toss all together. Cook down the liquid to preferred consistency; it should be somewhat gooey/creamy. Add green peas and white truffle oil and the remaining ounce of shredded Parmesan. Mix well and adjust salt and pepper to taste. Garnish with fried sage leaves and shaved Parmesan.

DOMENICA

123 BARONNE STREET
(504) 648-6020
DOMENICARESTAURANT.COM
EXECUTIVE CHEF: ALON SHAYA

Executive Chef Alon Shaya, partners with Chef John Besh in this contemporarily designed space—dark brown walls, chain-mail curtains, and giant brightly colored paintings—is a rock star. Alon's travels and culinary education across Italy helped him carve a brilliant menu of rustic Italian dishes, pizzas, pastas, salumi, and savory beignets.

The roasted cauliflower, a whole head with whipped feta, and the fried kale with lemon zest and Parmesan have a crazy cult following by even the most ardent of carnivores. The specially built pizza oven bakes up beautifully bubbled, slightly charred pies topped with house-made salumi, market vegetables, cheeses, and spices. Making a meal of a pizza, a vegetable side, and a bottle of wine from the well-curated list is the way most diners go, if they can pass up the big salumi and condiments board. Domenica gets creative with special coursed dinners held throughout the year and is packed for the half-price pizza Happy Hour. There are house-crafted fruit and herb cellos, cocktails, and joyful desserts like the Chocolate-Hazelnut Budino or seasonal fruit cobblers. Re-creating Domenica's pizzas takes skill and a wood-fired pizza oven, so Alon gave up one of his toothy pasta recipes with an earthy tender pork ragù, mille grazie.

Handmade Pasta with Mangalitsa Pork Ragù

This is a dish that reminds me of "family meal" in Italy. Halfway through the workday, we would all stop and sit down to lunch together. I remember when Fili, the sister of the chef I worked for, prepared this for us one day. It really hit me that Italians cherish the times when family and friends sit down together to break bread. Or, in this case, pasta.

(SERVES 6)

For the pasta:

10 ounces pasta flour, number 00

8 ounces ricotta

2 eggs

Salt to taste

Pinch of freshly grated nutmeg

For the ragù:

2 pounds bone-in shoulder of pork, preferably Mangalitsa

1 tablespoon kosher salt

1 teaspoon ground black pepper

¼ cup olive oil

¼ onion, chopped fine

1 carrot, peeled and chopped fine

2 stalks celery, chopped fine

1 clove garlic, chopped fine

1 cup peeled, cored, and diced tomatoes

1 cup dry red wine

1 quart water

¼ teaspoon ground cloves

½ teaspoon ground nutmeg

8 black peppercorns

2 sprigs rosemary

1 sprig oregano

2 bay leaves

For assembly:

2 tablespoons salt

6 cups pasta

2 tablespoons olive oil

2 cups pork ragù

1 cup good-quality tomato sauce

3 cups Tuscan kale, cleaned and ripped into large pieces

4 tablespoons dried red currants, reconstituted in pork broth

3 tablespoons cold unsalted butter

6 tablespoons grated Parmigiano-Reggiano

2 tablespoons extra virgin olive oil, for finishing

To make the pasta: Place flour on a wooden table or cutting board and make a well in the middle with your fingers. Add the ricotta, eggs, salt, and nutmeg to the middle. Using a fork, begin to work the wet ingredients into the dry ingredients until they all come together and form a dough. Knead the dough with your hands for about 8 to 10 minutes or until it looks smooth. Sprinkle a touch more flour on the work surface if the dough begins to stick. Let dough rest for 1 hour.

Using a rolling pin, roll out the dough in a large rectangle until it is ¼ inch thick. Using a pizza cutter, cut lengthwise into ½-inch strips. Then cut 1½-inch segments from each strip. You should now have rectangular pieces that are ¼ x ½ x 1½ inches. With your thumb, press each rectangle onto a gnocchi board and roll with a downward motion to form a hollow tube with the pasta so that the pasta curls over onto itself. If you don't have a gnocchi board, you can just press it on a wooden cutting board.

Once you have a good quantity made, dust with flour and place in a single layer on a baking sheet. Then you can wrap and freeze for future use.

To prepare the pork ragù: Preheat oven to 325 F. Season the pork shoulder with salt and pepper. In a large saucepan or Dutch oven, place the olive oil on high heat and wait until it begins to smoke. Add the seasoned pork. Reduce heat to medium. Brown the pork on all sides. Remove from the pan. Add the onion, carrot, celery, and garlic and cook over medium heat until golden brown. Add the tomatoes and wine and simmer until the wine reduces by half. Add the water, clove, nutmeg, peppercorns, rosemary, oregano, and bay leaves. Place the pork back in the pot. The liquid should barely cover the meat. Bring to a simmer

and cover the pot. Place in the oven for 2 to 3 hours or until tender. Allow to cool, then remove pork from the broth and pull all the meat off the bones. Cut meat into small pieces and return to the broth. (This can be done 2 days ahead.)

To assemble: In a large pot, bring 1 gallon of water and 2 tablespoons of salt to a rolling boil. Add the pasta and cook for 5 to 7 minutes until tender.

Meanwhile, heat a large sauté pan over medium heat. Place 2 tablespoons olive oil in the pan and heat until very hot. Add pork ragù, tomato sauce, kale, and currants. Simmer until the liquid in the pan has reduced by half. Add the pasta to the sauté pan and simmer until the sauce reduces and coats the pasta. Add the butter and the grated cheese. Taste for seasoning. After you plate the dish, sprinkle 2 tablespoons of very good extra virgin olive oil over it.

ARTS
&
WAREHOUSE
DISTRICT

American Sector

945 Magazine Street
(504) 528-1940
NATIONALWW2MUSEUM.ORG/AMERICAN-SECTOR
Executive Chef: Todd Pulsinelli

Another of Chef John Besh's restaurants, this one housed inside the World War II Museum serving retro food revisited for today. Executive Chef Todd Pulsinelli tweaks hamburgers, hot dogs, chicken and dumplings, meatloaf, and milkshakes by either shrinking their size (mini cheeseburgers with bacon-onion marmalade), tossing in local ingredients (Creole mustard appears in lots of sauces), or creatively reinventing delicious nostalgic dishes (Sloppy Joe made from slow-cooked short ribs). Foot-long hot dogs are handmade on the premises, fried chicken comes with Todd's latest batch of watermelon pickles for a crunchy sweet-sour companion, and there are even throwback Tiki cocktails generously poured. If a Sunday dinner ritual includes Chinese food, check out Todd's Duck Fried Rice studded with confit, breast, cracklin's and slow-poached duck egg.

CHAPPAPEELA DUCK FRIED RICE
(SERVES 4)

2 Peking ducks
1 cup salt, for confit
½ cup shaved garlic
2 cups duck fat
6 sprigs thyme
2 cups Louisiana jasmine rice
1½ cups English peas
1 tablespoon each sugar-salt mixture
¼ cup distilled white vinegar
4 duck eggs
1 tablespoon chopped shallot
1 teaspoon chopped garlic
1 teaspoon chopped fresh thyme
1 teaspoon turmeric
Salt and black pepper, to taste
1 tablespoon green onion

To make the duck confit: Butcher whole ducks; reserve breasts. Coat duck legs with salt and shaved garlic. Let cure for 24 hours. Rinse off salt and garlic mixture. Place duck legs in a pan and cover with duck fat and thyme sprigs. Cover pan with foil and bake in a 200°F oven for 3 hours, until meat pulls from bone. Cool in fat for 24 hours. Pick meat from bones.

To cook the rice: Rinse rice. Place in a medium pot, add enough water to cover rice by 1-inch, bring to a boil, and turn off direct heat. Seal pot and let sit for 15 minutes until rice is totally cooked. Fluff and cool down rice.

To prepare the peas: Shuck peas. Bring 3 cups of water to a boil in a medium pan with sugar-salt mixture. Add peas and blanch for approximately 90 seconds. Shock peas in blanch water with ice additive.

To poach the eggs: Heat 5 cups of water to 188°F. Add distilled vinegar. Crack eggs into water and let poach for 3 minutes. Cool water so the eggs stay warm.

To cook a duck breast: Trim excess fat off sides of breast; score skin with hatch marks. Set a sauté pan on medium heat, approximately 325°F. Salt breast on both sides and place in pan, skin side down. Render for 5 minutes on medium-low heat. Flip the breast and cook on the other side an additional 2 minutes. Let breast rest for 4 minutes before slicing.

To assemble: Sweat the shallots and garlic in the duck fat. Add rice and toast lightly. Use duck fat if rice is too dry. Add chopped thyme, turmeric, and 4 ounces shredded duck confit. Season with salt and pepper to taste. Add peas.

Place fried rice in the bottom of a large bowl. Slice duck breast on the bias. Shingle duck breast slices around and on top of the rice. Skim a duck egg from the poaching liquid and place in the center of the bowl. Finish with green onions and serve.

Cochon Butcher

930 Tchoupitoulas Street
(504) 588-7675
cochonbutcher.com
Executive Chefs: Donald Link and Stephen Stryjewski
Pastry Chef: Rhonda Ruckman

Chef Donald Link was the first to open a new restaurant as part of the post-Katrina recovery. In April 2006, Cochon started serving the citified country food of Chef Donald and partner Chef Stephen Stryjewski. Set in a restored New Orleans warehouse, the restaurant feels like gussied-up rusticity—all wood furnishings and soothing warm food colors on the walls. The food is Louisiana comfort that can begin with wood-fired oyster roast or a bowl of smoked duck and tasso gumbo before shifting to a citrusy-beefy-earthy mushroom salad with deep-fried beef jerky and lemon vinaigrette, and meandering over to rabbit and dumplings or namesake Louisiana cochon with roasted turnip, cabbage, and cracklin'. It's for these dishes and their dedication to New Orleans that the chefs won a James Beard Award. Donald and Steven planned to open a shop for retailing the fresh meats they house-butchered, and other foodstuffs they made, so, not long after Cochon, came Cochon Butcher—a sandwich counter, butcher shop, and wine bar, rolled into one. People fell head over heels for the house-cured sausages and meats, pickles, mustard, and Cochon Muffuletta (to name one popular sandwich). The bacon pralines became legendary, as did the chocolate chip cookies that one local lawyer–food writer swears are a secret weapon designed by pastry chef Rhonda Ruckman to keep him hooked. The savory dishes at Butcher may be heavenly, but Rhonda's devilishly delectable pastry is a huge draw.

BREAD & BUTTER PICKLES

(YIELDS 7 QUARTS)

2 cups salt

1½ gallons water

1½ gallons ice

11 pounds cucumbers, in ⅛-inch slices

10 cups cider vinegar

10 cups sugar

½ cup mustard seed

2 tablespoons celery seed

2 tablespoons turmeric

2 tablespoons black pepper, coarsely ground

2 tablespoons red pepper flakes

2½ pounds onions, thinly sliced

Make brine with salt and water. Chill. Add ice. Pour ice-filled brine over cucumbers. Soak overnight in refrigerator. Combine vinegar, sugar, and spices. Bring to boil to melt sugar. Pour pickle over drained cucumbers and onions. Place in sterilized jars. Process 10 minutes.

COCHON'S PB&J COOKIES

(YIELDS 2–3 DOZEN)

For the Ponchatoula strawberry jam:

3 pints strawberries, washed, hulled, halved
1¼ cups granulated sugar, divided
Pinch of salt
½ tablespoon apple pectin
Lime juice to taste

For the peanut butter cookie dough:

2½ cups unbleached all-purpose flour
½ teaspoon baking soda
½ teaspoon baking powder
1 teaspoon table salt
½ pound (2 sticks) unsalted butter
1 cup packed dark brown sugar
1 cup granulated sugar
1 cup smooth peanut butter
2 large eggs
2 teaspoons vanilla extract
1 cup roasted salted peanuts, chopped

To make the jam: Place strawberries, 1 cup sugar, and salt in a sauce pot over low heat and simmer. Stir well and cook until the mixture has reduced.

Mix ¼ cup sugar and the pectin in a bowl. Sprinkle pectin mixture over simmering berries while stirring to prevent any lumps. Bring mixture back to a boil and remove from heat. Stir in lime juice.

Transfer to a container and place plastic wrap directly on surface of jam. When cool, refrigerate until set or overnight.

To prepare the dough: Preheat oven to 350°F. Sift flour, baking soda, baking powder, and salt into a medium bowl. Set aside.

In bowl of electric mixer with paddle attachment, cream together butter and sugars. Beat until fluffy, about 5 minutes, stopping to scrape down bowl as necessary. Mix in peanut butter until fully incorporated, then eggs, one at a time, and vanilla. Mix dry ingredients into peanut butter mixture with a spatula. Add ground peanuts. Mix until just incorporated.

To make the cookies: Working with 1 tablespoon of dough at a time, place in cup molds and flatten slightly. Add a tablespoon of jam to the center of each. Top with another tablespoon of dough. Bake until cookies are puffed and brown along edges, 14 to 16 minutes. Cool cookies until set, and remove from molds. Enjoy!

Emeril's

800 Tchoupitoulas Street
(504) 528-9393
EMERILSRESTAURANTS.COM/EMERILS-NEW-ORLEANS
Chef de Cuisine: David Slater

Full disclosure, for ten years I was one of the writers for the Emerils.com blog. I adored working for Emeril and remember the days when he could be found sitting behind his paper-covered desk in the narrow home-base offices on Camp Street, eating a sandwich while plotting the future. Emeril is a hero, an innovator, and damn killer cook, with an even more amazing palate. He opened his flagship restaurant in 1990 on a street that had gone fallow, in an area that was all but dead. That kind of dice-rolling smarts, combined with talent, is why he is a star. He also knows how to find great chefs to curry for his empire. Emeril's restaurant kitchen is helmed by the lovely and sharp David Slater. Chef Dave is a chef's chef, liked by everyone in the industry. His easy nature and intensity (when required) help him navigate an insanely busy restaurant where the food has gone from upticked southern favorites to all kinds of ethnic interpretations and back around to original items again offered as part of Emeril's twentieth anniversary. Always in step with what and how people eat, chefs Emeril and Dave keep the menu fresh with local and regional produce, and of course locally sourced meats and seafoods. When they find a food item not from our region, bank on it that it's the best available. Pork fat may still rule, but Dave knows how to lighten things up, so he offered this crudo (raw) recipe.

Emeril's Scallop Crudo

RECIPE COURTESY EMERIL LAGASSE,
EMERIL'S FOOD OF LOVE PRODUCTIONS, 2008

(SERVES 4 AS APPETIZER)

5 Maine day-boat scallops

2 limes

1 (8-ounce) Yukon Gold potato, peeled

1 (8-ounce) red beet, peeled

2 oranges

1 lemon

2 red grapefruits

1/8 teaspoon orange zest

2 tablespoons sugar

1/2 teaspoon Dijon mustard

1/4 teaspoon prepared horseradish

3 tablespoons extra virgin olive oil

4 ounces thinly sliced guanciale

3 tablespoons American paddlefish caviar

2 tablespoons toasted pine nuts, for garnish

20 baby arugula leaves

12 thin slices radish

12 thin slices jalapeño

Slice each scallop crosswise into 4 thin slices. Squeeze the juice of 1 lime over the sliced scallops and allow them to marinate for 10 to 15 minutes in the refrigerator.

Using a Japanese spiral slicer, slice the potato and then the beet. Store each in a separate bowl of water in the refrigerator until ready to use.

Juice 1 orange, lemon, lime, and grapefruit; there should be about 1 cup of juice. Pour the juice into a medium saucepan and bring to a boil over high heat. Once the juice boils, reduce the heat to medium-low and stir in the zest and sugar. Steadily simmer the juice, stirring occasionally, until it has reduced to 3 tablespoons, about 25 minutes.

In a small mixing bowl, combine the juice reduction with the Dijon mustard and prepared horseradish. Slowly whisk in the olive oil until the mixture is emulsified. Set aside.

Remove the rind and the pith from the remaining grapefruit and orange. Using a paring knife, remove all of the segments and set aside.

Assemble the dishes on 4 cold plates. Remove the beets from the water and pat dry. Arrange 1/4 cup of the beets on each plate. Evenly divide the scallops over the beets and then drizzle 1 tablespoon of the vinaigrette over each plate. Place 2 grapefruit segments and 2 orange segments around each plate. Divide the guanciale evenly into 4 servings and place around each plate. Remove the potatoes from the water and pat dry; place 1/4 cup of potato over each plate. Place 2 teaspoons of caviar, in separate piles, over the potatoes, and sprinkle 1 teaspoon of pine nuts evenly over each dish. Arrange 5 baby arugula leaves on each dish and top with 3 slices each of radish and jalapeño.

RENÉ BISTROT

700 TCHOUPITOULAS STREET
(504) 613-2350
RENEBISTROTNEWORLEANS.COM
EXECUTIVE CHEF: RENÉ BAJEUX

René Bajeux is hands-down one of the most interesting, smart, well-read chefs, ever, and he cooks like a man possessed. Obsessed with books on culinary history and the latest gossip, he's one of those chefs who is enormously fun to be around. Chef René's New Orleans story is a complicated route of twists and turns that can be summed up as follows: René's been in the kitchen since he was fourteen, and after many years cooking in restaurants (his own and others'), hotels, and resorts, he is home at last in his current self-named restaurant on Tchoupitoulas Street in Marriott's Renaissance New Orleans

Arts Hotel. The food is classic and contemporary French with some Alsatian and tropical island notes. Fans hankering for René's French onion soup will be pleased to find it on the menu along with new creations and perfectly prepared French bistro fare. In his heavily accented English, René says, "René Bistrot is a French bistro with an American passport." New Orleans gives him a stamp of approval.

Basque Seafood Ragout

(SERVES 6–8)

1 pound raw Chaurice (chorizo) sausage
1 large yellow onion, diced
1 fennel bulb, diced
1 red bell pepper, diced
1 tablespoon chopped garlic
1 tablespoon saffron
1 tablespoon dried thyme
1 tablespoon dried tarragon
1 tablespoon crushed red pepper
1 cup dry chardonnay
1 gallon shellfish or seafood stock
2 medium tomatoes, stemmed and diced
1 cup cooked cannellini beans
12 mussels
12 clams
12 Laughing Bird or Gulf shrimp

Brown chorizo sausage, then sauté onion, fennel, and bell pepper until lightly browned. Add garlic, saffron, dried herbs, and crushed red pepper, then sauté 1 minute. Deglaze with chardonnay. Add shellfish stock, and bring to a boil. Reduce heat and simmer until reduced by one-quarter. Add tomatoes and cannellini beans.

Place mussels, clams, and shrimp in a hot 2-quart stockpot and ladle warm broth over them. Simmer until mussels and clams have opened and shrimp have cooked thoroughly.

LEMONGRASS CHEESECAKE

(SERVES 12)

2½ pounds bar cream cheese, at room temperature

1½ cups sugar

1 teaspoon finely grated lemon zest

4 stalks lemongrass, juiced

½ teaspoon coarse salt

4 large eggs

1 cup sour cream

2 tablespoons mango puree

12 banana slices

Note: Photo below shows cheesecake "potted." It can also be served as a single slice.

Using an electric mixer, beat cream cheese on medium until smooth, scraping down sides of

bowl. Gradually add sugar, beating until fluffy. Beat in lemon zest and lemongrass juice, and salt. Beat in eggs slowly, one at a time, scraping down bowl after each addition. Beat in sour cream.

Preheat oven to 325°F. Line a 9-inch round cake pan with parchment paper and butter the sides. Pour in the batter, and set the cake pan in a larger baking pan to form a bain-marie. Pour boiling water into the larger pan to come halfway up the side of the cake pan.

Bake until just set in center, 1 hour. Remove cake pan from water; Unmold and then let cool completely. Cover with mango puree. Caramelize the banana slices and place on top.

Rivista

BREAKINGBREAD-LISA.BLOGSPOT.COM
CRESCENTCITYFARMERSMARKET.ORG
EXECUTIVE CHEF: LISA BARBATO

First I fell in love with Rivista's buttery, flaky, herbaceous tomato tarts and then I fell in love with Lisa. Lisa is a cook's cook, an incredibly industrious and hardworking pastry chef, who doesn't mess around, though she refers to herself as "the anti-baker," relying more on feel, sight, scent, and taste than on a scale. She has worked the pastry station at some of the city's most important restaurants, including Anne Kearney's storied Peristyle and the Brennan family's Mr. B's Bistro, and in the post–August 2005 restaurant landscape she did a stint at the short-lived Alberta's. Her plated desserts have graced magazine covers, and her special-occasion cakes bring tears of joy. Lisa has serious passion for all things Italian and French, so at Christmas there is panettone and during Mardi Gras there are French (puff pastry and almond paste) and New Orleans traditional (brioche style) King Cakes. Lisa became a regular fixture at Saturday's Crescent City Farmers Market in 2006, and since then has amassed a big fan base. Everything Lisa makes is from scratch, hand rolled, hand cut, filled and perfect. People call market managers to ask specifically about Lisa, and when she sells out of a particularly favored item, it's all sad faces, slumped shoulders, and promises to make it to the market earlier next week so as not to miss out. The core of her pastry case includes croissants (plain, almond, and chocolate), regular and whole wheat scones, bagels, muffins, fruit turnovers, savory turnovers, a tender Danish dough wrapped around lightly sweetened cream cheese filling, and those tarts, those damned addictive tomato tarts. I can't quit them—or Rivista.

TOMATO TARTLETS ON HOMEMADE PUFF PASTRY

(YIELDS 12)

For puff pastry:

1 cup all-purpose flour
2 cups bread flour
2 teaspoons salt
1 tablespoon sugar
1 pound unsalted butter, at room temperature
1 cup cold water

For pesto (makes 1 cup):

4 cups fresh basil leaves
⅓ cups walnuts (optional)
2 cloves garlic

½ cup grated Parmesan cheese
1 teaspoon salt
½ cup olive oil (not extra virgin)

For tartlet topping:

¼ cup pesto
1 cup ricotta cheese
2 medium ripe tomatoes
1 cup grated Parmesan cheese

To make puff pastry: In the bowl of an electric mixer, place the flours, salt, sugar, and ¼ pound (1 stick) butter.

Add cold water and mix with the dough hook until a ball forms. Do not overmix. Turn out ball and wrap in cling film. Refrigerate for at least 6 hours or overnight.

Press the remaining ¾ pound of butter between two sheets of plastic wrap and form into a ¼-inch-thick square that's 4 x 4 inches. The butter must be softened but not too soft.

Once the dough has rested 6 hours or overnight, roll it out into a 6 x 6-inch square. Unwrap the butter block and lay it diagonally on the dough square. Fold in the edges, envelope style, then fold the resulting square in half to make a rectangle. Brush away any excess flour, wrap in plastic, and refrigerate for 25 minutes. Once rested in the refrigerator, roll out the dough into a 6 x 18-inch rectangle.

Fold each of the outer one-thirds over the center one-third to make a 6-inch square, then fold in half again to make a rectangle. Wrap and refrigerate for another 25 minutes.

Remove from the refrigerator and repeat the roll-and-fold one more time. Wrap well in plastic and refrigerate for at least 6 hours. This method creates all those delicious flaky layers.

Remove dough from refrigerator. Roll into a 16 x 12-inch rectangle. Using a 4-inch cookie cutter or pastry ring, cut 12 circles. Make a circle depression in each dough round using a slightly smaller (3-inch) ring. Be careful not to cut through the dough. This smaller ring will create an "edge" to hold the filling.

Place pastry rounds on a parchment-lined baking sheet and wrap well. Refrigerate for 1 hour or freeze to be used within one month.

To make pesto: Combine basil, nuts (if using), garlic, cheese, and salt in a blender or food processor. Pulse until mixed well. Add olive oil and pulse until paste forms.

To assemble and bake: Preheat oven to 425°F. Remove prepared dough from refrigerator. Top each dough round with a teaspoon each of pesto and ricotta. Top with a thin slice of tomato and sprinkle with 1 to 2 teaspoons of Parmesan cheese. Bake for 20 minutes, rotating once, until puff pastry is golden brown. Eat warm or let come to room temperature. Best eaten the day it's made.

FARMERS MARKETS

New Orleans farmers markets are more than a place to grab fresh local produce, they function as an event, a social gathering, a hub of information, and more. Most markets also offer music, cooking demonstrations, kids' activities, book signings, and prepared foods made from farmer-vendor produce.

Of course the original New Orleans farmers market was the French Market in the French Quarter, near the Old U.S. Mint. Historians tell us that the market site was a Native American trading place before New Orleans was New Orleans. It operated as a burgeoning public market, and by the end of the nineteenth century was a cultural collective where French, English, Spanish, German, Italian, Creole, and African languages could be heard. Early grocery entrepreneurs began with market stalls. The market flourished with butchers and fishmongers, cheese vendors and greengrocers from Saint Bernard Parish who trucked in produce to sell. That spawned roving street vendors and other spin-off markets that evolved citywide. In the 1930s and 1940s,

public markets gave way to supermarkets and lost ground along with shoppers. By the mid-1990s the French Market had become a tourist destination for the flea market crammed with kitschy T-shirts, sunglasses, and knockoff designer watches.

However, across the country there was a resurgence of farmers markets, and New Orleans was not to be left out. In 1995 Richard McCarthy, executive director of Market Umbrella, and a dedicated group of like-minded folks launched the Crescent City Farmers Market with a mission to "cultivate the field of public markets, for public good." The first market opened that year in September, on Saturdays, and was an almost immediate success. From there came a Tuesday market at what was once a shopping mall called Uptown Square, a short-lived Wednesday market (in the work-in-progress renovation of the French Market), and a Thursday late-afternoon market in the parking area of a restored Mid-City factory, now an apartment building. Of course, August 2005's Hurricane Katrina put a halt to the markets, and for a moment no one was sure whether the open-air markets would return.

Despite the devastation both emotional and physical, New Orleanians sought, actually needed, a marketplace to convene, socialize, learn, and shop. Weary though they were, the founders and some new, determined, and dedicated believers helped the Crescent City Farmers Market, the French Market, and a slew of other public markets return to the landscape.

Today the list of farmers markets is bigger and better than ever. They exist beyond the Orleans Parish lines and make for a great day-trip.

THE FRENCH MARKET (daily, 10 a.m. to 6 p.m.)—Back and much more gussied up with covered areas and an indoor "kitchen stage" for cooking demonstrations, it is also the home of many food-related festivals. The produce is there along with locally made food products (hot sauces, jams, pickles, seasonings, and such). Crafts have replaced most of the junk.

CRESCENT CITY FARMERS MARKET (Tuesday Uptown Square market, 9 a.m. to 1 p.m.; Thursday Mid-City market, 3 p.m. to 7 p.m., at the parking lot of American Can Co.; Saturday market, 8 a.m. to noon, in downtown New Orleans on the corner of Girod & Magazine Streets)—The markets offer fresh produce, seafood, fish, meats, chicken, prepared foods, herbs, pastry, pesto, dairy, and native plants.

HOLLYGROVE MARKET & FARM (Tuesday, noon to 6 p.m., and Saturday and Sunday, 10 a.m. to 2 p.m., at 8301 Olive Street)—Seasonal produce grown throughout the region and food items.

COVINGTON FARMERS MARKET (Wednesday, 10 a.m. to 2 p.m., and Saturday, 8 a.m. to noon, at the Covington Trailhead, 419 N. New Hampshire)—For fresh produce, local goods, plants and prepared foods.

CAMELLIA CITY MARKET (Saturday, 8 a.m. to noon, at the City Parking Lot at Robert Street and Front Street, Slidell)—Farmers market offering regionally grown fresh produce, "value added" goods and foods.

GRETNA FARMERS MARKET (Saturday, 8:30 a.m. to 12:30 p.m., at Gretna Market Place, between 3rd and 4th Streets at 300 Huey P. Long Avenue, Gretna)—Rain-or-shine Gretna Farmers Market features more than thirty vendors offering a broad range of fruits and vegetables, meats and flowers.

SANKOFA FARMERS MARKET (Saturday, 10 a.m. to 2 p.m., at 3500 Saint Claude Avenue, New Orleans)—Featuring vendors from across South Louisiana with locally grown produce, specialty foods, cooking demonstrations by the Sankofa HEAL Project students, musical performances, kids' activities, and community health screenings.

VIETNAMESE FARMERS MARKET (Saturday, 6 a.m. to 9 a.m., at 14401 Alcee Fortier Boulevard, New Orleans East)—Twenty or more vendors set up blankets spread with produce, herbs, homemade tofu, eggs, and live chickens and ducks for sale. The courtyard houses shops selling Vietnamese baked goods and groceries.

WESTWEGO FARMERS AND FISHERIES MARKET (Saturday, 8:30 a.m. to 12:30 p.m., on Sala Avenue at Fourth Street, Westwego)—More than fifty booths selling citrus, seafood, farm fresh eggs, jellies, pickles, fresh baked bread, cakes, pies, prepared foods, and crafts.

Root

200 Julia Street
(504) 252-9480
ROOTNOLA.COM
Chef/Owner: Phillip Lopez; Co-Owner: Maximilian Ortiz

Chef Phillip Lopez is a culinary mad scientist. Yes, he uses chemicals and techniques to create foods and seemingly impossible dish compositions, and yes, he uses these modern methods every day, with big success. A puff of smoke blows from a cigar box opened tableside to reveal masterfully cooked scallops and vegetables. Icy "dippin' dot" avocado pearls appear atop a salad of seared tuna, compressed watermelon, feta cubes, and torn fresh herbs. Beets are roasted and tossed with berries, pistachios, and blue cheese crumbles, then finished with house-cured smoky "face bacon." Cauliflower, baby eggplant, potatoes, spices, and herbs combine with a textural crunch from handmade corn nuts in Phillip's Aloo Gobi. There are rice noodles made from local Jazzmen Rice that come mounded in a bowl for a spin on Vietnamese bun; piles of fresh vegetables from local farms and markets are prepped raw, or roasted or pickled; meat cabinets store mind-numbing amounts of charcuterie and sausages; condiments like strawberry mustard or the kitchen's own ketchup are pushed into little toothpaste tubes and sent out on plates. The menus are insanely stunning; it's difficult deciding where to begin or end.

The design of Root's interior is modern, modern, with warm natural wood touches. Co-owner and business partner Max Ortiz has front-of-house operations down to an art. He runs the restaurant with warmth and efficiency, assisted by an amazing staff. The bar offerings are bold, fun, and easy drinking. The essence of Root is that it reflects the core of what Max and Phillip aim to accomplish in the restaurant world . . . everything they can. For this book, the guys have shared Phillip's riff on chicken wings with a cheeky name, and one of his genius desserts that explores layers of flavor. "Eat. Here. Now." isn't just their motto, it's a command worth following.

"KFC" Korean Fried Chicken Wings

(SERVES 3)

For the Vietnamese-style kimchi (yields 3–4 cups):

1 head green cabbage
2 leeks, white part only
3 jumbo carrots
5 jalapeños
5 Thai chili peppers
2 cups rice wine vinegar
2 cups granulated sugar

For the pepper jelly glaze (yields 3 cups):

3 cups apricot jelly
1 cup finely diced tricolor peppers
¼ cup honey
½ cup chopped ginger
½ cup chopped garlic
4 tablespoons chili garlic paste (sambal oelek)
¼ cup soy sauce
1 cup mirin rice wine
15 dashes Tabasco sauce

For the chicken wings:

2 sprigs lemongrass
5 garlic cloves, whole
2 cups soy sauce
1½ cups sliced fresh ginger
1 cup lime leaves
2 cups salt
18 jumbo chicken wings
3 cups nonglutinous rice flour
Oil for deep-frying
6 ounces pepper jelly glaze
1 tablespoon toasted white sesame seeds
2–3 cups Vietnamese-style kimchi
1 tablespoon chopped chives

To make the kimchi: Slice cabbage into ribbons and place in a large plastic container. Cut leeks in half lengthwise, wash well, cut off root ends, and place in container with cabbage. Peel carrots, slice thinly lengthwise using mandoline, and add to cabbage and leeks. Slice jalapeños on the bias and add to vegetables, along with whole Thai chilies. In a medium-sized pot pour rice wine vinegar, sugar, and 2 cups water and bring to a rapid boil. Pour hot vinegar mixture over vegetables and cover tightly with plastic wrap. Let sit out at room temperature for at least 2 hours, then refrigerate.

To make the jelly: Place all ingredients in a pot and simmer. Stir occasionally to prevent scorching. Reduce by one-quarter and remove from heat. Let cool.

To prepare chicken wings: Bring 1 gallon water to a boil. Add lemongrass, garlic, soy sauce, ginger, lime leaves, and salt and cook for 5 to 8 minutes.

Turn down to a simmer. Place chicken wings in seasoned water and blanch for about 3 minutes only; this will help release some fat from the skin and make the skin tighter for frying. Remove with slotted spoon and shock in ice water. Chicken may now be reserved for later use.

To finish the wings: Toss the wings in rice flour to coat well. Submerge wings in hot oil at 350°F and cook for about 7 minutes or until fully cooked inside. Place hot wings in a clean mixing bowl and coat with pepper jelly glaze.

Place wings on serving plates and sprinkle with toasted white sesame. Place kimchi next to wings and garnish with chopped chives.

Sweet Corn Caramel Flan, Salted Corn & Caramel Ice Cream with "Crackerjacks"

(SERVES 6)

For the ice cream (yield: 1 quart):

2 cups half-and-half
1½ cups sugar
15 egg yolks
2 cups sweet corn milk (corn kernels steeped in milk, then pureed and strained)
1 quart heavy cream
Pinch of kosher salt

For the flan:

1 quart heavy cream
1 cup corn milk
8 egg yolks
2 cups granulated sugar, divided

For the "crackerjacks":

1 quart popped popcorn
¼ cup Spanish peanuts, skins removed
1 tablespoon unsalted butter
½ cup light brown sugar
¼ cup Steen's cane syrup
¼ cup light corn syrup
Creole spice, to taste

For the Moroccan spice (yields 1 cup):

1 ounce freshly ground black pepper
2 ounces freshly ground star anise
1 ounce freshly ground green cardamom
⅔ ounce freshly ground cinnamon
2 ounces granulated sugar

For assembly:

6 sweet corn and caramel flans
2 cups "crackerjacks"
9 ounces Sweet Corn and Caramel ice cream
1 tablespoon Moroccan spice
3 ounces caramel sauce
Mint leaves for garnish

To make the ice cream: Bring half-and-half and sugar to a boil and remove from heat. Whisk egg yolks to break them up and then whisk a little bit of the hot liquid into the yolks slowly. Continue adding warm mixture until all is incorporated. Return to a pan and then add corn milk. Cook to 170°F. Remove from heat, stir in cream and salt, and chill. Process in an ice cream maker according to manufacturer's instructions. Transfer to a suitable container and place in the freezer.

To make the flan: In a large mixing bowl combine heavy cream, corn milk, egg yolks, and 1 cup sugar to make the flan base. Blend using hand blender until all sugar is incorporated and partially dissolved. Set aside.

In a small pot combine remaining 1 cup sugar and ¼ cup water and cook over medium heat. When sugar turns an amber color, pour 1 ounce of the caramel into each of 6 (5-ounce) ramekins. Twirl dish so the bottom is fully coated. Let caramel cool to room temperature.

Preheat oven to 300°F. Pour 4 ounces of flan base in each ramekin. Set ramekins in a baking pan and fill the pan three-quarters with room temperature water. Cover baking pan with aluminum foil and bake for 2 hours. Remove ramekins from water bath and let cool.

To make the "crackerjacks": Place popcorn and peanuts in a heat-resistant bowl in a 250°F oven.

In a heavy pot, combine butter, sugar, cane syrup, and corn syrup. Bring to a boil and cook until the sugar mixture reaches hard crack stage at about 260°F. Remove warm popcorn and nuts from oven and pour hot sugar mixture over them. Stir vigorously with a wooden spoon to coat fully. Spread on a baking sheet lined with a nonstick silicone mat. As it cools, sprinkle Creole spice over mixture to season.

To make the Moroccan spice: Grind all spices separately. Combine with sugar in a bowl, and mix well. Transfer to a jar with a tight-fitting lid. Store in a cool place away from the light.

To plate: Unmold each flan from its baking dish and drain excess caramel. Place flan randomly on a plate. Top flan with ⅓ cup "crackerjacks." Sprinkle Moroccan spice on plate and drizzle caramel sauce in random spots. Finish with a small scoop of Sweet Corn and Caramel ice cream. Garnish with mint leaves.

Recipe Index

General Index

About the Author

Lorin Gaudin has passion for all things food and drink. With a bachelor's degree in Theatre from Loyola University of New Orleans, and a culinary diploma from the Ritz-Escoffier in Paris, she parlayed her education to become a food editor/reporter for national, regional, and local publications, as well as local television and radio stations. Lorin is a contributing editor/writer for the *New York Post*, *Where New Orleans*, GoNola.com, and CITYEATS.COM. She is the creator-founder of FiveOhFork, specializing in culinary social media/web content. Lorin can be found on IMDb.com and her alter ego New Orleans Food Goddess can be followed on Twitter and "liked" on Facebook, where she posts delicious raves and the occasional rant.

About the Photographer

Born in Mid-City New Orleans, Romney Caruso used the distinctiveness of his surroundings to train his eye in the art of alluring image creation. Through dedication to his craft, his skill garnered him numerous awards and brought him international attention. But true to the roots of the environment he grew up in, he kept focus on the things that truly matter: love of family, great music, and superior food!

For years, Romney has brought to light the indelible imagery of New Orleans' cuisine. The richness of the pageantry and flair that accompanies this very unique gastronomy can only be matched with Romney's unforgettable photography that practically brings the taste of the food right off the page. This is accomplished through his genuine homegrown love of food, paired with his incomparable skill at capturing light and displaying the beauty of a true culinary masterpiece. His greatest joy is derived from working with the people he has met on his sessions including famous chefs, restaurateurs, and individuals from various walks of life.

—*Ade Herbert*